The Student's Guide to

Passing Exams

RICHARD BURNS

**KOGAN
PAGE**

First published in 1995 as *Pass Exams and Write Top Essays*
Stirling Press, PO Box 39, Old Noarlunga, South Australia 5168
This edition published by Kogan Page Limited 1997

Kogan Page Limited
120 Pentonville Road
London N1 9JN

© Stirling Books, 1995

British Library Cataloguing in Publication Data

A CIP record for this book is available from the British Library.

ISBN 0 7494 2247 5

Typeset by Kogan Page Ltd
Printed and bound in Great Britain by Clays Ltd, St Ives plc

Contents

Introduction

Academic performance is like a sporting event. Success relies on four essential elements:

- *determination*
- *competition*
- *ambition*
- *communication*.

These driving forces are developed and enhanced by ability and aptitude, technique and skill, and experience – knowing how and what to do and when to do it to maximise your results. As in sports, the key is intelligent and consistent training backed up by practice and the growth of confidence.

In any academic race, the performance of an individual is profoundly affected by self-confidence. Knowing exactly what is expected of you in an exam, or when writing that important assessment essay, provides a key foundation to confidence – nothing chokes up the mind and erodes capability like uncertainty, confusion or misunderstanding.

But there is a more vital element of exam success and writing essays that earn top marks – skill in communication. All the elements above depend primarily on the outlook of the individual and his or her determination and application. Effective communication – the skill needed to write clearly, briefly and logically – not to mention accurately – can be taught. That is the purpose of this book.

Most students who succeed in their academic ambitions will eventually find employment (usually in a profession) where the ability to communicate effectively, either by word of mouth or in writing, will be an essential part of their responsibilities. What you learn in the sometimes harsh and competitive process of passing exams and essay writing will never be lost or redundant. The better your communication skills the higher you will almost certainly climb up the professional, commercial or even political ladder.

And central to the ability to communicate well is the ability to persuade – to arrange facts logically in a manner that convinces the listener or reader and even changes their previous opinion. This was once termed 'rhetoric', a word that has come to mean empty sayings designed to mislead or deceive rather than inform and persuade. Indeed many politicians and international speakers have abandoned rhetorical skills in favour of the 30-second soundbite. Not too many years ago, however, rhetoric was a university subject, regarded highly as a means of applying knowledge to best effect. An author practised the art of rhetoric when writing, a public speaker was judged on the quality of his or her rhetorical ability.

We look at how you can use rhetoric in Chapter 4, but here let us consider one of the last great traditional exponents of the art, Sir Winston Churchill, the British wartime leader. Love him or hate him, and there were many on both sides, no one would deny his skills in oratory or literature. By the use of rhetorical technique and device, he could sway emotions, call on prejudices or impel people to act. As far as I know, no one ever said of the British leader Churchill that, 'patriotism is the last refuge of a scoundrel'. His opponent, the Nazi leader Adolph Hitler, also applied the skills of rhetoric, leading a whole nation into a blind alley of warfare and mass killing such was the power of his persuasive ability.

Answering exam questions or writing essays may seem far removed from the great communicators of history, but the principles they applied to persuading listeners or readers are the same as you need to apply. A good persuader who knows the facts and marshals them into a strong argument, such that the examiner is persuaded that he or she is competent and has mastered the topic of the question, will get good marks. The student in effect is applying the same techniques that have made great leaders successful.

Lesson one, then, is:

Fact + Argument = Persuasion

Your aim is to persuade the examiner or essay marker that you know your stuff. If your argument is strong and the presentation such that the facts are clear and logically arranged, you will obviously win marks over those students whose presentation is muddled and based on a weak argument, however well they may remember the salient facts.

Parrots, contrary to some people's belief, are not the best academic performers. Clear thinkers are. To think clearly, you have to learn to order your mind and refine study technique to avoid all the puff and nonsense and stay on the main track. Waffling through when you don't really know the answer fools no one and only wastes everyone's time, especially yours. If more students at school and university had mastered the principles and techniques of good communication there would be far fewer boring speakers, dense legal documents, tedious parliamentary prattle and third-rate media reportage. If this book can help you steam through your studies with outstanding results, it will also do much to help you in the next phase of your life in the real world of competition, promotion and effective communication.

Society is changing rapidly. The advent of computers, and the ever-widening sophistication of global communications, makes it vital that you can express yourself clearly and forcefully. More than ever before, the world rests on foundations of words. Words may be the basis of information but they are also the tools of beguilers and deceivers, the propagandists and spin doctors, the 'hidden persuaders' who want us to buy or think or do what they believe is appropriate – whether for commercial, political or ideological reasons. By mastering language and its use you will protect yourself from deception because you will be able to see beyond the honeyed or twisted words to the argument and the motive beneath.

Enough of the theory, let's get down to work.

We start in the first chapter by putting down some foundations – how to learn effectively and without wasting unnecessary effort. But we also consider this in the context of keeping yourself in shape physically, too. The process of spending long, sedentary hours straining your eyes over books and notes does little for your physical well-being. So we suggest that mind and body are one and both require training, not straining.

Another important concept comes to the fore here. Trust your own mind, a super computer, to do a whole lot of work that you do not need to drag out into the bright light of consciousness until

3

the time comes. The mind, this amazing computer-like attribute, has a vast capacity which is unused in most people. We suggest some ways you can make better use of your hardware by applying better software to the intellectual processes.

Notetaking (that chore!) is examined, too, with suggestions for making the process relevant rather than a dull ritual. We consider the motivation of interest and the point at which the mind computer crashes when boredom strikes.

In the second chapter we set targets and goals and establish a timetable to bring some order and structure into the ongoing process of training for the big events. This chapter sets the scene for relating to the teachers, gaining an overview of where the course(s) is leading and why, and backing up contact hours with the wealth of other resources in educational institutions and public facilities. We also suggest you learn to type, because this is as essential a skill as handwriting was in the recent past.

In Chapter 3 we get down to the nitty-gritty – essay writing technique. The lessons to be learned here underpin all forms of student assessment. The principles are no more than have been taught to generations of writers and journalists (with varying degrees of success) but they form the basis of clear communication. Part of this process concerns the way in which words are set out on a page, on presentation to facilitate understanding and quick comprehension. We touch on the rationale of research, principles of a good writing style, even the way in which exam or essay markers react to the form of your answers.

From there we look in Chapter 4 at making language serve the task for which it is being used, and how the technicalities or spelling and grammar are essential elements of the skills you need. Words are seen as tools used to cultivate understanding – but they have to be ordered in such a way that even paragraph structure becomes an important aspect of the free flowing of facts. Punctuation, too, makes your meaning certain and allows your reader time to breathe and absorb your argument.

We show you how to run a clear and compelling argument – just as you would have to do in a debating team – by systematically countering objections or controversy. You'll learn to summarise and reinforce your answers and arguments so the central points are not forgotten and the overall object of your communication is sustained to the very last word.

In Chapter 5 comes the business of preparing for exams – developing the right state of mind, understanding what is needed from you and dealing with the limitations of physical well-being, exam nerves, fatigue and sheer blind panic when faced with baffling questions. Keeping your cool is an essential attribute, too. In Chapter 6 we review the 'science' of swatting – recapitulating and ordering everything you have learned before the exam so you can demonstrate proficiency during it without wasting time or driving the examiner into a deep depression. We look at how to organise your notes, recall essential information as you need it (and not before), and the time-scale in which all this hard work should be done to enhance your performance for the best possible results.

Finally, the big day comes. How will you react and perform against whatever hurdles you encounter? The advice in Chapter 7 is set out to maximise your capacity and minimise your uncertainty. It covers what to do when you are faced with the reality of the exam paper, how to make the best of your time and confront your shortcomings. Self-discipline here comes to the fore – you have the ability to control the exam timetable and fulfil all the requirements in a cool and rational way. Beating the 'block' and fighting fatigue also feature in this essential advice.

In the final chapter we assess what you have learned and your performance so far, and see where this fits into what may prove to be long years of exams, essays, seminar papers and even 40,000 word theses before you are finished. Words and yet more words to be produced, pruned and propagated. Another important point comes to the fore here – developing the ability to handle criticism, even though you may resent it, and learn from it.

To conclude, we set out in summary the ten secrets of exam success, the three essential elements of a good essay and offer some pointers on gaining marks the easy way.

We suggest you take this book in small doses – say a chapter a day at the beginning of your academic year – so you can lay down the right basis for effective study and learning. If, however, you have only bought the book a month before the first exam, you may just have to swallow it whole. Whichever way you choose, you have nothing to lose and everything to gain because few teachers today, especially at university level, have time to get these points across. They are concerned primarily with filling the pot. How to apply the contents, in this school of thought, is up to you.

1. Laying the Foundations

Motivation

Learning, real learning, is founded on a need to know – on the motivation to discover information essential to some aspect of your life. The problem faced by many school and tertiary students is that they *don't* need to know much of what is being thrust upon them. How you overcome this fundamental difficulty, in the long run, will determine your level of academic attainment.

Confront a young person with a particular problem, or a personal difficulty, and they will soak up information like a sponge. More to the point they will *retain* that knowledge, probably for life.

Think of someone you know who speaks a second language, particularly a language learnt in the country where it is spoken. A decade, two decades, after they last spoke that tongue they still retain the ability to communicate with a surprisingly large vocabulary. Compare this retention with those who had an unwanted language forced on them at school. One was a live language based on a pressing need to communicate. The other was a 'dead' exercise lacking any real motivation to impose the self-discipline necessary.

There is another element here, however, which involves the teachers. The school subjects in which I excelled were in major part taught by outstanding teachers who fired my imagination and interest and gave me a lifelong appreciation of their discipline. To achieve good exam results or write effective essays about these topics was never a problem for me – the material just flowed from my subconscious mind in an ordered and compelling form.

Other competitive or personal forms of motivation may spur success, too. I had a geography teacher who was rude, sarcastic and so bored with his subject that he inspired no interest in it at all. In the final year of school, I withdrew from his course. This made him angry and even more bitingly sarcastic.

'Whether you attend my lessons or not, I'm going to enter you for the matriculation exam. If you don't sit for it, you'll simply get a failure recorded on your university entrance certificate,' was his response.

This was as unreasonable as it was unjust. However, the last thing I needed on my matriculation certificate was a 'Fail' so, unbeknown to the teacher, I did some reading on my own account. That year the topics were Australia and New Zealand and, coincidentally, my family was moving to Australia later that year. Even with this motive that weary teacher could not inspire any interest in me. But for some reason I retained everything I could discover about the country and flew through the final exam with good marks. The geography teacher never forgave me for this wicked breach of educational integrity, but I have always savoured my victory.

Motivation takes many forms. Some students may want to better the efforts of peers or siblings, others may be driven to fulfil the ambitions of parents, or even show contempt by succeeding where failure was endlessly predicted. Some may be fired by personal ambition, others may try to compensate for shortcomings on the sports field or their inability to relate to the opposite sex. Strange forces drive us powerfully at some periods of our lives and the years of adolescence are particularly prone to intentions that may be understood only in part.

Whatever fires *you* up, value the advantage because it is the key to learning and retention. This is the basis of *intelligent* learning, the need to know.

Where you are able to choose the subjects you study, select those that have this essential foundation and you will gain a head start. If, however, you are compelled to take, say, a maths subject or study a language to gain appropriate qualifications, and neither of these subjects inspires any interest, the first step is to build a direct link with your personal motivations.

If, for example, you were required to learn another language, try at an early stage to visit the country and develop a feeling for the people and their language. This will give you an invaluable appreciation of the pronunciation, the sounds, which are the structural basis of that language. If a visit is impossible, find photographs of the country in the library, watch TV films about it, follow the news and political events, talk with native speakers, involve yourself with the culture of that people to the widest possible extent.

As you encounter the subtleties of the language, you will have a greater breadth of understanding and interest. Learning any language, even a 'close' European tongue, is a labour of love, and you need to be motivated. The best motivation of all is a real prospect of having to use that language to communicate.

A student compelled to take a maths subject, particularly if he or she is not numerate, has a harder task. Again, you need to have a motive for learning. One way is to look for a holiday job or gain work experience in a commercial setting such as a shop where you have to handle money and use mathematical processes like calculating percentages. Any function in the real world using maths will round out your potential interest by creating a need for that skill.

You could look for computer games that make use of maths ability, or set about building a boat or even draw up rough plans for a home extension – anything that demands mathematical skill. Once you begin to relate the theory to the practice you will begin to change your attitude to the subject and break down some of that initial resistance.

Study techniques

Let us assume you have crossed these bridges, the school term is about to start, and you have to consider the day-to-day realities of study technique.

Avoid red herrings

In my experience, too many students lose the track and wander off into the hinterland of a subject. Though not sufficiently motivated to learn, they nevertheless chase irrelevant and often useless information to the detriment of the central aim of the course. As a consequence, when essay or exam times come, they present information which may be comprehensive but is not to the point.

Timetable your studying

Learning is a gradual process, like building a house. Brick on brick of information is built on the foundations until you are ready to put on the roof and tie the whole structure together. If you only start laying foundations four weeks from an important exam you have little chance of doing justice to the topic.

Allocate your workload in the light of all your commitments

Sport, your social life, peer relationships, parental and extended family demands, recreation and relaxation all have an important part to play in your life. If you can form an overall picture of what must be achieved by the end of the school or academic year, and distribute that work across the total time available, the study process will be much more effective. And you are much more likely to retain what you have learned.

Choose your subject topics carefully

You may have the option to choose specific topics within your subject, and you should focus on those that for you have relevance, strong interest and practical application. The age-old question, 'What do you want to do (or be) in the future?' can be difficult to answer when you are still at school, or even when you get to university. Often the things that motivated you as a teenager will be cast aside when you reach your mid-twenties, so the idea is to keep as many doors open as possible.

Seek advice

Parents, older siblings, friends, teachers, tutors and careers advisers may be all too eager to drench you in advice, much of it specious. If you go looking for help, make sure the adviser is qualified to give *sound* advice. Some people may very well make you aware of facts, views and options you had not considered.

Develop a positive attitude to studying

The key to effective study is organising both yourself and the various learning tasks to attain the best long-term benefit. Some people are disorganised, haphazard and thrive on chaos; but somehow out of all this confusion there emerges a coherent pattern of work. In others chaos always reigns and nothing worthwhile ever emerges, despite the latent abilities of the student. A degree of personal order is part of the self-discipline necessary for success. A muddled mind too often produces messy arguments.

Keep your study materials in order

Know where your books are and how to find information without wasting time on a tedious search. For example, tick off index references you may need again so you don't have to check each entry repeatedly. If you have access to a personal computer in the home, and you are computer literate, consider how you might use this powerful tool to make study easier. (More on this later.)

Set aside places where you can concentrate

You need to study away from distractions like younger siblings or TV so you can focus your mind on the task you have set yourself. It helps to aid concentration if you can study somewhere set aside for the purpose, whether this is part of your bedroom or the library. Sustained concentration is important in retaining information, but the attention span of some individuals is often quite short. So be aware of your limitations and work within your capacity to be effective.

Set yourself reasonable and realisable goals

Such goals are more easily achievable. If you are not making out, restructure your study practices until you get the good results you expect.

Health and well-being

The study demands of the final years of school and tertiary education are akin to training for a major sporting event. In this case, however, you not only have to develop intellectual fitness but maintain the physical condition and stamina necessary to stay the course. Health concerns – diet, exercise, not burning too much midnight oil, avoiding the byways of drugs or smoking or the many other routes to debilitation – are as important for academic achievement as for athletic prowess.

This need to get yourself into shape physically and intellectually, and even emotionally, is part of your academic workload. Mind and body are part of the whole living organism – you neglect one at the expense of the other. A dumb athlete will seldom achieve much, an unfit student who lacks the staying power to handle the demands of study will also find the going hard.

That is not to say people who are handicapped or at some physical disadvantage cannot succeed. Rather, it means that they have to invest more effort in the intellectual process to make the grade.

Planning for exercise and recreation is an important part of organising your study comprehensively to allocate time for everything, especially adequate sleep and relaxation. It has always seemed to me unfair that an adult can go to work, complete the tasks demanded of him or her during the working day and return home with time to put their feet up in the evenings or on weekends. But the unfortunate school or university student must do homework or extend on the educational institution's contact hours by home study, and this sharply reduces the time available for socialising, keeping fit or just flopping out in front of the TV. Yet these activities are as vital as a good diet for health and well-being and will often determine the overall capacity of the student.

Trusting your own mind

We will assume you have considered all this background and are facing the first term with a mixture of enthusiasm and apprehension. Where do you start? The first point to digest concerns your computer – not the hardware sitting in the spare bedroom but your *mind*, you *own* personal computer (PC). Trusted and used with confidence, it is a remarkable organ. It has possibilities of which you are probably unaware and which you may never use unless you learn to draw on its computing power.

Think about that other and grossly inferior piece of electronic hardware in the spare bedroom. Unless you know how to make the best use of the software installed on a computer you will not be able to maximise its resources. With experience, however, you will be able to play tunes on the machine and produce some surprising results. The mind is different.

You don't have to be trained to use it, rather you have to teach yourself to trust it and then get out of the way. The moment you start intruding into the computing process by dragging everything 'onto the screen' – into consciousness – you slow down the processing and mess up the result. However, when you sit down to write an essay or, more to the point, take an exam, you must be able to find the right files and open them in order. And, in the case of your mind, there's no file manager to search through the archives for you to locate the right bit.

Civilisation can be seen as a result of the human mind developing consciousness beyond that of the spontaneity of an animal on all fours. The ability to reason – to use one's head rather than one's heart – has lifted the human animal to higher ability and attainment.

Yet it is often the case that intuition (just 'knowing') comes up with the right answer, while the conscious mind flounders in a sea of contradictions and counter-arguments. Too often I've seen students sitting outside an examination room trying frantically to remember some apparently essential fact, and getting into a panic state over their inability to get it all up on the screen at once. If only they had learned how to trust their minds to deliver the information when required, or trigger it as part of a sequential argument, they would have been less stressed and more competent.

We'll have more to say on this essential point in Chapter 6.

The art of making notes

Once you start your course, you face a problem from day one – what do I do about taking notes? You have probably sat and watched the ardent few who take down almost every word religiously, to the point where they are not listening, they are simply transcribing for future assimilation. Why not listen first and note only the key points? These will bring back to consciousness the teacher or lecturer's point. The ardent notetakers don't trust their own minds to sort out the wheat from the chaff and they face a daunting task when it comes to later organisation and revision, not least in deciphering their own handwriting.

The bulk of what is said in any one lesson or lecture is usually developmental and does not need to be retained in any formal sense. It is a means to an end. The end in this case is comprehension – understanding the subject and being able to use the information offered to arrive at your own conclusions. By trying to get every detail down on paper you are denying yourself the ability to listen, to order the data in your mind and to reason. You do not have time to think about the topic, raise objections or counter-arguments, and sustain a level of critical ability. You become a recording device rather than a rational listener. Learning is about developing and maximising skills and latent abilities as you develop an appreciation of a wider culture, not regurgitating facts.

Some points made by the teacher do need to be noted, however, such as a chemical formula, a heading that summarises an important argument, a name or a date. Think of your notes as *triggers* rather than a personal textbook. There will almost certainly be some form of printed material to back up the course, but even this will have to be gutted and filleted later. So don't add another whole layer of flather on top of that.

One student I know who achieved exceptional results prided herself on never taking a single note. She used to say it would all be underlined in the undergraduate textbooks in the library if it was significant and she needed to listen to the teacher's argument to understand what was being said within the broader context of the subject. There was no way this could be done properly if she didn't listen at the time.

This student had a secret weapon. After a lecture she went to the library, found a quiet corner, and jotted down in simple form a series of headings that summarised the content. She then kept this in date order so she could refer to it later if she needed to remember some fact or specific viewpoint.

Learning what you need to know

One problem with notetaking, and listening, is that you don't know what you need to hear. This applies to both the broader appreciation of the subject and the narrow objective of passing exams or gaining good assessments or essay marks, and is precisely why promiscuous notetaking is pointless. Until you know the structure and thrust of the course, and the teacher's aims, you don't have any sense of direction, nothing to steer by. There may be course summaries or outlines which will help to give an overall picture and delineate both the road and the destination, but this won't show you how all this accords with your needs and objectives. To learn what you need to hear you have to fix in your own mind the direction you are taking and the extent to which the information proffered will fire your interests and motivation. If it does not fulfil your expectations, you will be bored. If it does or if it expands on them, you will be carried along by enthusiasm and learning will follow automatically.

Having resolved this critical issue, it is time to be practical.

Organising information

You are faced with a stream of data that are assailing your mind and cluttering up your notebooks. On top of this, you are required to read or carry out various exercises to demonstrate the extent to which you are assimilating the material that is being loaded on to you. Your first task is to set up a system that enables you to organise the written information.

You need a looseleaf folder for lesson or lecture notes so that each page of headings, 'triggers' and essential detail can be placed in sequence or where relevant. Take what notes you must on, say, an A4 size lined pad so that each page can be placed in the looseleaf binder where you most need it for reference or later revision. A well organised student could set up a contents list for each topic or section of the binder and even build up an index for locating key materials.

If you don't take detailed notes you should write neatly in longhand and underline key words or phrases to assist later recall. Illegible notes are worthless, so it is important to discipline your handwriting from the start. (My handwriting was unreadable, so I was forced to develop a new longhand for a task which was clear and easy to read. This took two or three weeks, and my handwriting eventually reverted to its original primitive form, but the result was rewarding at the time.)

File notes daily, or at worst weekly, but never, ever let them accumulate in a disorganised heap. Order, we have said, is part of the discipline necessary to succeed academically, in exactly the same way that self-discipline underpins success in any sporting or competitive endeavour. If you want to succeed, make the effort.

The easiest notes to use are those that are laid out carefully without a conservationist's attitude to paper use:

- key headings at the top of each page or paragraph;
- abbreviated notes and points beneath;
- some words underlined where they are vital for an understanding of the topic.

These notes will form the basis of a system used later to prepare for exams and ensure adequate recall of all the relevant information, so we have to ensure at the outset that the essential information is *recorded and easy to find*.

Creating your own data bank

If you are able to use a PC you can set out your notes in a form that is easy to retrieve. However, remember to back up everything you do or keep hard copies in a looseleaf folder. The advantage of the computer over hard copy looseleaf notes is that you can retrieve specific topics more easily and quickly. Most word-processing software offers search and find functions that should enable you to locate data, particularly where you use keywords to organise your material. When you have to write an essay you can scroll through your keywords and bring on to the screen all the facts and trigger points you need. Your mind, at this point, is more than able to do the rest – if you will trust it to take over.

What you have after all this is two interlocking data banks – the trigger points in your binder or on the computer, and your mind. This has a more impressive computing capability, because it orders and rationalises information according to your needs and personal responses in a way that a machine cannot. The two must interface (to maintain the metaphor) and so interact that learning is simplified and maximised.

2. Defining the Workload

Set targets and goals

Start by carving the school or academic year into bite-sized chunks. At best, you are going to have about nine months to embrace the coursework, complete assignments or essays and prepare for exams. Into this you also have to fit your social life, sporting interests and sufficient recreation.

First, you will need details of the course(s) you are undertaking and dates for essay submissions and exams. Once you know exactly what will be expected of you over the year you can set yourself targets and goals to be reached by specific dates. The first secret of successful academic performance is to be on top of the game – not a victim of haphazard reactions to pressures applied by teachers or tutors.

An effective student, invariably, is one who is sufficiently organised to tackle the workload systematically and meet deadlines without stress.

Avoid over-reaching yourself

To do this, you have to know your capabilities and be realistic about the time it will take you to complete the work, and when you need to hand it in.

That's easier said than done. Most people have trouble accounting for all the interruptions and unexpected events that are bound to occur, so their estimates of completion dates tend to be wildly awry at times. Illness may set you back a week, there may be family commitments you had not remembered, or you may not have adequately allowed for a whole range of minor demands on your time. You could easily find yourself running out of time no matter how well you planned at the outset. Allow for all these

– and other, unimaginable – contingencies. Build in to your timetable a lot more time than you think you need.

If the worst doesn't happen and you finish early, regard this as a bonus and do some of the things you had to cast aside earlier. If every conceivable problem does arise – you can't get a textbook you need, a family member is taken seriously ill, or you start to run out of puff towards the end of the year, you will have made allowances and your work can still be completed on time.

It is only human to say to yourself that what you don't need to do today you can do tomorrow – procrastination. We all do it. The problem is that some people keep putting things off indefinitely and find it ever more difficult to get down to serious work in time. There's only one way to deal with this problem effectively – set yourself weekly and monthly targets and stick to them. If, through no fault of your own, you miss one of these deadlines, catch up at the earliest opportunity. Don't allow your whole schedule to slip further and further or you will run up against an exhausting and counter-productive log jam at the worst possible time – immediately before you have to take exams or submit major essays.

It is better to load up the earlier part of the year with extra work when you are fresh and enthusiastic, and build up a cushion, or reserve of time, for the latter part of the year when you are starting to feel tired and tense. Academic work, and exams in particular, cause a lot of stress for many young people. Keeping your workload as light as possible in the weeks running up to exams can do much to alleviate that stress and any feeling of constant 'pressure to perform'. Planning, realistic planning, makes this possible.

Focus on key issues

One reason that some students become stressed and anxious as the year progresses is that they try to do too much. They think they have to cover the whole syllabus in minute detail and spend time on many needless forays into the academic undergrowth when they should have focused on the main theme. Allocate the work to be done by sorting out the key issues and topics, the areas on which you will be tested or assessed, and relegate to a second order all the subsidiary material. You can also reduce your workload significantly by filtering out the dross to avoid getting caught up in unimportant issues.

Get to know your teachers

Obviously you will need guidance from teachers, tutors or lecturers to select the areas on which you should focus. As well as studying course outlines, communicate with your teachers and anyone in a position to guide you to make the right judgements.

Apart from providing you with invaluable information and detail, getting to know the teachers puts a face to your name and creates, however superficially, a relationship which will prove invaluable later in the year if you need help. For my part, I would much rather be able to relate a name to a particular student so I can round out my judgement of his or her work by some knowledge of their broader abilities. In some cases, it is better for the exam or essay marker not to have any familiarity with the student, to ensure consistency of marking or so that favouritism does not intrude.

The aim of good marking from the teachers' standpoint is arriving at a fair assessment of the students' capabilities and knowledge. If a poor result belies a student's real potential, a teacher can act to correct that anomaly rather than letting it ruin a person's career.

Your lifestyle

In planning the year you need to arrange convenient living and perhaps travelling facilities. You must have suitable study space, quiet and easy access to libraries and other resources. Over my years on campus I found the university library one of the best locations for study, for two reasons. First, the information was there for the asking, or finding, and invariably up to date. Second, there was a serious 'work atmosphere'. By this I mean that everyone there (with occasional rude exceptions) had their heads down and were getting on with the job studiously, and this prompted me to do likewise.

Find out the times when public institutions (such as museums and local government offices) can be used, what happens on weekends or public holidays, and when public use is least to facilitate a quiet working environment.

Now for three golden rules.

1. Build into your study plans one day a week when you have nothing to do with study. Do no reading, no essay writing, nothing that even suggests an academic purpose. By clearing your mind for a day each week and having a total break you will return to your task refreshed and clear-headed (provided you don't spend the day off in pursuit of some debilitating excess).

2. If you get very tired and are unable to concentrate, take a break. Take a whole day off or more if necessary, to give your batteries a chance to recharge. Working when you are exhausted is unproductive. Better to rest first, then do the work in half the time and twice as efficiently.

3. If you are unfortunate enough to get flu or any other infection, by all means use the time spent recovering for reading, organising your notes or whatever, but don't force yourself back to work too soon. Many infections leave you excessively tired, during the recuperation phase. By pushing yourself too hard, too soon, you only delay your recovery, the work probably won't be worth much and you may well succumb to another bug.

Three other essentials

Learn to type

Today's library and university resources are almost all computerised, and access to data stored in data banks (both on PCs and mainframe systems) is vital. If you can handle a keyboard accurately and reasonably quickly, you will not only save time but give yourself a much wider range of information sources, especially through the so-called information superhighway (the Internet).

But you need to be able to type for another important reason.

Learn computer skills

Word-processing on a PC saves essay preparation time because there is no need to retype or rewrite corrected material. You simply call the file up on to the screen, make whatever changes you want and then print the revised copy, maybe only one page out of five. The time saving is substantial and you can hold the final version on hard or floppy disk for later use. Some of the search, index sorting and layout functions of a good software program could be useful, too. 'Find' facilities can help you to get specific information quickly without having to waste reading time.

As an aid to study and essay preparation the PC is indispensible. So if for some reason you are not computer literate or cannot keyboard, commence your studies by mastering this tool. Most schools and further or higher educational institutions have training courses in computer use. These are very popular and you should enrol as early as possible. Learning to access and use the system well doesn't take long in these days of user friendliness but keyboard skills take time to refine. Even if you are slow to start with, persevere, do all your work on the computer and you will soon find the process becoming automatic.

Beware the fanatic who insists everything has to be done by the book. Most people can manage to get good work out of a computer with little theoretical understanding of the system or the software. And you don't have to touchtype (type with all your fingers) to gain reasonable speed, whatever the experts say. Many two-finger typists can rattle along at a good rate, good enough to keep pace with their thoughts anyway. One important word of warning: computers crash. Make back-up disks of all your work so that, in the unhappy event that the system lets you down (and it will one day), you have a copy of *all* your work.

Identify sources of information

Locate and familiarise yourself with *all* the information resources in your academic and wider community. Sometimes material in a major public library is more accessible than in a school or university library. This may be because the demand for the book or resource is not as great, or because the material is presented in a more basic form.

If you don't know how to get the best out of a library, go to the enquiries desk and ask a librarian to talk you through everything you need to know and show you how to use card or computer-based catalogues. These are usually straightforward, but a few tricks of the trade can greatly speed up your work. Don't be shy or afraid to ask, however elementary you think your question may be.

In pinning down information sources never overlook people or contemporary accounts. If, for example, your work in modern history covered the period of the Great Depression and World War II, there are still many people around who were there and remember their experiences clearly. Firsthand sources are often much more exciting and revealing than dry textbook accounts of raw facts. An essay rounded out by reports of firsthand experience of particular events will fascinate the reader and score good marks in comparison with a dull parade of dates and dreary academic assessments.

You can also expand history sources by looking beyond the set texts. For the period referred to above, many popular magazines and newspapers are available in bound editions or on microfiche, and these offer detailed accounts of events. In terms of social history from around the mid-1850s to, say, the 1970s, the humorous publication *Punch* contains a wealth of superb material, much of it sharply critical. Bound editions of old journals like the *Tatler* give fascinating accounts of fashions and social mores of the late nineteenth and early twentieth centuries.

In contemporary terms students who are computer literate enough to get on to the Internet have the world (and possibly some big bills) at their fingertips because they can access university and library resources worldwide. They can also communicate with people anywhere in the world and share information (at a price).

As someone who has been subjected to the inanities and plagiarised tripe served up by one generation in exam papers and essays, I have to comment that a student who shows initiative in finding new sources and presenting his or her material in a fresh way wins out every time. A marker's heart warms to such devotees. You put the examiner to sleep at your peril.

3. Essay Writing Technique

Let's get down to work. For many students the first major test of knowledge and ability is likely to be an essay based on a topic that covers work already done in the classroom or in lectures. But, in addition to reinforcing the key points learned so far, the function of the essay is to build on the basic foundations laid previously.

The essay writer, therefore, is setting out to achieve two developmental goals – order and structure knowledge already gained, and extending that information laterally to broaden understanding of the subject. By compelling the essay writer to go looking for additional and interesting information, the teacher wants creative input from the student. This creativity comes in two ways.

Effort applied in seeking new and relevant information familiarises the student with the specific resources available in his or her own institution, in other libraries or in other sources about that topic area. The degree of imagination the student exhibits in this search may tell the teacher a lot about his or her involvement in the subject, and more generally, about his or her academic potential.

Here comes the difficulty, however. If you are going to communicate by way of the written word you have first to master whatever shortcomings you may have in essay writing technique and writing style. Most students reaching university level or in tertiary training should have mastered the fundamental principles of spelling, grammar and punctuation. But we are still going to look at them here.

Spelling, grammar and punctuation

Spelling

Spelling is not a fixed process. In many English-speaking countries there is conflict between British and American spellings, particularly the inclusion of the letter '*u*' in words ending in '*–our*' and the use of 'z' in words ending in '–ize'. The debate can even come down to unattractive propositions like 'sox'. Newspaper and TV advertising does not help in this conflict and newspapers, notably the tabloids, but even some of the better quality productions (the broadsheets), seem to have given up any responsibility for preserving standards. There is even a wide variation of spellings in most dictionaries.

An important point, however, is that spelling may be as much a matter of style and regional usage as what is correct. Government bodies and all printed publications have what is called a style manual that sets out the preferred spellings for commonly used words. This is done to ensure consistency in presentation throughout all publications. Book publishers may have the same problem, particularly where an author spells the same word more than one way in a manuscript. Pedantic teachers sometimes insist on correcting words not spelled according to a particular convention. More generally the view is that spelling matters less than knowledge and comprehension, and that the refinements of language use should not be allowed to get in the way of assessing the student's real abilities.

The contrary school of thought is that formal language *does* matter because, without effective and clear communication, students cannot necessarily reveal what they know and the way in which their minds are working. On balance, I would have to subscribe to the second view, because the purpose of this book is to get you, the reader, performing to the very best of your ability to maximise marks and your academic potential. Language use in this view places the techniques of communication within the cultural heritage we all receive as part of the process of growing up.

There are good spellers, those who just 'see' whether a word is correctly spelled by its shape or the configuration of letters. These people, when they meet a new word or one they are unsure about, tend to reach for the dictionary – thereby fixing the correct form of the word in their minds. Then there are mediocre spellers, who have to work at spelling and who, generally, like misspellings to be corrected so they can get it right. These people generally have to *learn* to spell. Finally, there are the bad spellers, who either don't care or who have a condition such as dyslexia which makes spelling and word recognition difficult.

There is one more point to make about spelling before we go on to consider solutions. Many people have spelling quirks or constantly mispronounce words. For years I used to say 'warrantry' until someone pointed out my mistake. Even then, I had to make a considerable effort to overcome the unnecessary *r*. When we type, we may also make repeated mistakes.

Every student would be well advised to face up to his or her spelling competence. A mediocre or bad speller has a huge advantage on his or her forebears because most computer word-processing programs now have a 'spellcheck' (but make sure the spellings recommended are in the correct form of British or American usage for your educational institution).

Using a spellcheck is effective only where a misspelled word does not accidentally match another word in the machine's memory. So spellchecking an essay on the computer may only reveal *some* of the errors. These may be actual misspellings or simply typographical errors caused by hitting the wrong key.

There are also a number of simple handheld spelling checkers with computerised dictionaries on the market – another good reason to learn to type competently as soon as possible. In principle, learning to type does much to formalise language use and presentation.

These computerised spellcheckers cannot usually be used in exams, however, so you really have to tackle your spelling shortcomings on your own. You can do this by

1. becoming conscious of the words you repeatedly misspell; and

2. correcting your understanding of words you constantly use in the wrong context.

Grammar

Grammar, the way in which words are structured and arranged, is a key to strong communication, yet the traditional patterns of use are now in disarray as English-speaking communities interpenetrate and travel. Many grammatical forms are evolving – language is a dynamic process that is in constant change – as people from different countries, regions and social backgrounds communicate.

For those people who were taught meticulously to use only 'correct' grammar every mistake, however trivial, grates. More liberal listeners are philosophical about the inconsistencies and take the view that effective communication is the bottom line.

Accepting that language is in constant flux, one cannot communicate clearly and unambiguously without a set of rules roughly equivalent to the Highway Code. If we all conform to the Code, and stop at the traffic lights or obey the rational traffic laws, there will be fewer accidents and much less misunderstanding.

Social concerns arise here, too. A young person from one background, when exhorted to speak or write correctly (differently) by a teacher from a different world, may be placed in conflict both with his peers and his family. Take the classic case of the correct use of adverbs, words that describe verbs. Mostly, these take '–ly' on the end. I run quick*ly*, she left hurried*ly*, he argued incessant*ly*. But many do not, and this has led to confusion for some users. He jumped high. She ran fast. They fell down. As a consequence there is widespread misuse of adverbs along the lines of *they ran quick.*

This raises another issue. Given that language is evolving, at what point does a grammatical error become common usage and therefore correct? For example, pedants cringe at split infinitives, but these are now commonplace in all major newspapers, on radio stations and in general conversation. For that matter, they are not even technically incorrect, they just sound awkward and intrude on clear speech. The infinitive of a verb is its basic form – to jump, to run, to think, to fly. If you insert an adverb between the *to* and its verb, you are splitting this form – hence the term 'split infinitive': to quickly run, to carefully think and, the most famous of all, 'to boldly go'.

Curiously, most people who drop the '–ly' from adverbs placed after the verb in common use include it in a split infinitive. We can't give you a full rundown of English grammar here because this is not intended to be a grammar textbook. Good grammar is important for our purposes only so far as it clarifies and enhances written work. This makes it worth pursuing to improve the technique of communication.

There is another aspect of this question. In the old British class system in particular (one replicated in many former colonies), a whole system of barriers and boundaries to delineate classes was built – language use (particularly grammar), table conduct, forms of greeting, dress codes and rules of etiquette and social presentation to name just some. For anyone from 'humble origins' the wider world of social intercourse was fraught with all kinds of stumbling blocks. These, therefore, served to keep the 'upstarts' down, and those 'in the know' up.

These are all the wrong reasons for language rules. You need to sift out the social paraphernalia from the rationale of effective language use – and that is where good exam performers and essay writers come in.

Punctuation

Now here's a minefield of little dots and dashes. If a teacher launches into a diatribe about clauses and relative clauses and the strict rules of punctuation (especially commas), little else will get done for the year. There are some simple principles, however, that will lift your game to the point where your exact meaning is not compromised by the adjoining words.

A well-written essay is dependent on punctuation to clarify what is being said and make it easier for the reader to absorb. If you have ever seen a legal document of old without a comma from start to finish, you will grasp how valuable punctuation is. But we must also punctuate to communicate precisely and more effectively, not just to conform to a set of rules. One can sometimes break the rules where the result makes the point more forcefully – as advertising copy-writers are wont to do, sometimes with less than pleasing results.

So, the primary purpose of punctuation is to make your meaning exact, and the common comma is a vital tool. We look at other questions, like paragraph structure, in Chapter 4, but a quick few words on the comma here. Some teachers, despairing of teaching the proper use of commas to students who have never learnt formal grammar, use rules of thumb – like putting in a comma wherever you would like to take a breath. That is not good enough. A comma separates ideas and propositions in a statement, a sentence, and keeps like with like so that the reader knows precisely what is intended by the writer.

Commas also serve to break up a flow of ideas into bite-sized pieces so they can be grasped more easily. Take a few pages of this book and examine the use of commas analytically to see what can be achieved using this principle. But don't fall into the trap now occupied by many journalists of putting commas exactly where they don't belong, thereby destroying comprehension and making a nonsense of the flow of words.

If you are still unsure, you can always resort to the time-worn technique of reading your work aloud. You should discern the need for commas that way (even if you don't need to take a breath).

Before you start writing

Do your research systematically

Assess where you need to go beyond your notes and study materials provided by the teacher or lecturer to research new information, new facts. Simply regurgitating the well-digested stuff will not do. An essay is intended to stretch your mind. It is a framework on which you can take the topic and pull it in all directions until you get a much rounder and more satisfying picture of the issues involved. Boring and passive reruns of old facts and tired clichés just won't do.

If you are going for top marks, something much more exciting and rewarding is needed – and the only way you will achieve this is through thorough and careful research. The material you need could come from books, journal articles, media reports (wherein facts may be at a premium), conversations with enlightened people, tape recordings or interviews, oral history... whatever. Tell the examiner/marker something he or she didn't know...

Consider the principles of marking

Put yourself in the position of essay marker, marking your own contribution. How are you going to assess the standard? You can pick out facts and place a tick in the margin for representation of every essential point. Or you can read the whole piece and assess whether the writer has presented a convincing argument. Or you can give marks for comprehension, scope, logical exposition, relevance or any other criteria that seem to fit the task. But at the end of the day any assessment will have a measure of subjectivity, whatever standards and rules are imposed on the assessors.

This is why exam papers and essays are often marked by more than one person. The average of the marks may give a fairer picture of the student's performance where this is done. It also lessens the possibility of personalities and even vendettas intruding on the process of marking. If marking always has a subjective element, that is that each individual marker will see things differently, then you can gain marks by winning over the marker with the goodwill that flows from (and to) a good essay, well presented, without fluff and nonsense.

Now to the essay in its entirety.

Writing the essay

Understand the topic

Read the question or topic carefully, then read it again, and be quite sure that your answer will present the information that the essay setter wants from you. I remember a university lecturer who set an ambiguous essay topic then, when his students chose one interpretation, decided he preferred the alternative and proceeded to fail all his students. Apart from this deception, he was on trial for lack of clarity, too. There was a near riot, of course, and after formal complaints the essay was ignored in the final results. The only way one could beat a topic like that would be to answer both options, which no doubt was what the lecturer intended. He did, however, teach his students to read the topic carefully and thoughtfully.

Start at the beginning

From the beginning, go to the end, and there stop! That is a near quotation from the poet C. Day Lewis' *The Otterbury Incident*. It may sound like a statement of the obvious, but it is good advice when you consider how many people seem to start in the middle, or the end or anywhere *but* the beginning. Your first sentence needs to state the topic, and the rest of the introductory paragraph should set out the background to the subject. Then you are ready to jump into the nitty-gritty.

Keep it short, clear and relevant

Be economical with words. For some unimaginable reason, many people confronted with a keyboard, or an essay question, lapse into a form of convoluted language they would never dream of using if they were speaking to their friends. The language you use at the club may not be appropriate for a more formal presentation of your knowledge, but a concise and clear explanation is far preferable to never using a short word when you can think of a longer one, a technique adhered to by too many lawyers, public servants and medical practitioners.

A preferable form of the rule is *never* use a long word where a short word is *better*.

The issue of relevance is more complex. To decide what is germane to the issue you are debating, and to assess relevance, you have to know your subject. This is because you have to understand *why* it is relevant before you can decide that it really is. So the test of relevance is in principle a comprehensive test of your grasp of the subject, and more specifically of the essay topic. If a statement is not relevant, that is it in no way supports your argument or says anything anyone would really want to know when discussing the topic, cut it out.

Some essay writers accumulate words for their own sake. They set out to fill the required length of the piece with sufficient words, however ordered, to fulfil their own expectations. Whether those words are wholly relevant is not an issue in this mode of thinking. It would be better to write at half the length but cover all the relevant issues logically than waffle out a 'required' length. Most essay markers abhor waffle and have wide experience in dealing with it harshly.

Layout and presentation

Small, spidery handwriting reaching from top to bottom and within a millimetre of either side of the paper presents a galling task of decoding for the reader. Use clear-cut paragraphs, not too long and of varying lengths, adequate punctuation and uncomplicated sentences – all presented with some regard for the reader's comfort. Leave lots of white space, use a good pen (or, preferably, a typescript) and have wide margins at the top, bottom and on both sides. At least the assessor will start off in a positive frame of mind.

Keep the reader awake

Teachers and lecturers have been there, done it and seen it all before, so many times in some cases that there is little stimulus or excitement left in the chore of marking. Many exam or essay markers may be performing this chore at times when they are not running in top gear. If the essay writer wants to get the message through that he or she is competent and has a wide grasp of the topic, their first task is to keep the marker awake. And an excellent way to do this is to include something unexpected.

This could range from a surprising conclusion, a brilliant insight, a poetic piece of colourful writing or, in a more mundane sense, a *readable* essay. State your case, summarise your points, vary the typefaces (as has been done in this book), break up your statements into digestible lumps and (maybe) use some of the tried and tested techniques of professional writers. These include a startling first sentence, a relevant and revealing story or personal anecdote, a compelling quotation. Do not, however, resort to the banal, like those companies that head up their advertisements in newspapers:

SEX... now I've got your attention...

Stick to the facts

This is the golden rule of admissible evidence and goes beyond the earlier comments about relevance. Only use facts that support your argument or throw light on the topic. Discard everything else, no matter how much trouble you experienced digging it out from the small print of an indigestible encyclopedia. Facts, facts and more facts, woven into a comprehensive argument that carries the reader to an unavoidable conclusion – that is the formula for success.

Make it all your own work

The great advantage of an essay is that it is a reflective and considered piece of prose that can be checked and commented on by others before submission. One student I know supplemented his income at university by writing essays for his less confident peers and got better marks/assessments for them than he was able to achieve himself. Just what this tells us, I'm not sure. The wheel of fortune, perhaps.

But be warned. Most teachers and tutors soon gain an idea of the capabilities of their students, and a scintillating essay from one who has failed to sparkle in lessons or tutorials will raise immediate suspicion. Plagiarism, presenting the work of others as your own, is neither honest nor educational (other than in what it says about the character of the plagiariser). If the purpose of gaining an education is to do just that, passing in essays written by someone else will not advance your interests because it will only work in the early days. Once you get down to the serious work, you will be very vulnerable if you were too lazy to do the job for yourself in the beginning.

By far the best way to develop a good writing style is to be conscious of good writing in others. Your favourite authors, able newspaper or magazine columnists, the classic literature of Shakespeare and Dickens even, can teach you so much about the art of expression, of creative communication.

4. Secrets of Effective Communication

In this chapter we go more deeply into the techniques by which you can get your point across, reveal the depth of your knowledge, help others to read what you write and persuade the reader to agree wholeheartedly with your viewpoint.

So much of what is written in the world today is plain boring. If a student can learn to write sparkling essays or answer questions intelligently and so sustain the interest of the reader, he or she will convey an enthusiasm for the subject and an involvement that goes beyond a pot being filled with facts. If the reader is interested (in this case the examiner or essay marker) he or she will assimilate what is being said and that must mean more marks, provided that what is said is accurate, reasonable and persuasive.

This 'persuasion' in part is about convincing the examiner/marker that you know your stuff and have taken the trouble to go beyond the bare requirements of the classroom or lecture notes. How, you groan helplessly, can this be done?

Not only must the text be readable and interesting, it has to sustain the reader's interest throughout. The reader in this case is a person well steeped in the subject matter. He or she has not only heard it all before but has probably been subjected to endless, sound or idiotic interpretations (or misinterpretations) of the facts to the point where much hair may have been pulled out in despair and blood pressure has no doubt risen alarmingly. For a teacher at any level of learning – secondary or tertiary – there's nothing more galling than spending a year teaching someone some essential material only to have it handed back in a garbled and misstated form. So your first responsibility is to *get it right.*

When we look more closely at the science of recapping in Chapter 6 you will see how we can work to get all the misunderstandings out of the subject and focus on the hard facts that matter. By thinking about the topic and applying the judgement developed during the period of study you are then able to interpret the facts correctly and make a much more complex presentation of them.

The last thing you need to do is upset the examiner or assessor. To avoid this, remember the points made in Chapter 3 about layout and presentation, refine your English language usage and don't let *bad* communication get in the way of what you know and wish to say.

Paint a picture or tell a story

Now let us consider some of the tricks of the trade used by journalists and writers the world over. There is nothing difficult about these, and even an elementary appreciation of some of these techniques will relieve the tedium of exam papers and essays from the reader's viewpoint. Bald facts presented sequentially can be boring if they are not wrapped up in a more attractive parcel. Much of this tedium can be relieved if you present your information by painting a picture or telling a story. How do you do that?

To paint a word picture, you go beyond the bare bones of the facts and add colour, light and shade, supplementary information that rounds out and places the bare facts in context. If, for example, you were answering a question about one of the great musical composers – Beethoven, say – you could add colour by noting his deafness and the age at which he lost his hearing, speculate on how he might have been able to continue composing by 'hearing' the music in his head, consider the frustrations of never being able to hear his work performed, and so on.

Suddenly, this 'colour' lifts the answer or essay from the mundane to the fascinating, especially where you can dig up some little-known information as a bonus.

Another well-used technique is to present information in the context of a story. Say you are asked, for example, to write about the problems of economic development in Bangladesh. Instead of cataloguing a chain of events, why not invent an imaginary family of perhaps three generations and create a fictional world based on the realities of Third World life in which you record their lives, problems and economic frustrations? You could show how each generation has faced a different set of circumstances as the family has moved from subsistence on rural land to urban life, how some members of the family have been educated and obtained well-paid jobs in the cities while others have been further deprived by losing their land to big landlords.

Behind every essay question there is usually a story to tell, whether it is a question about the discovery of antibiotics, an essay about paper manufacturing (forest conservation) or a seminar presentation about the mating behaviour of the death-watch beetle (the destruction of historical buildings). Wherever there are facts, it is possible to arrange these nuggets like polished stones in a diamond ring if you apply some imagination and determination to the prospect.

If you are going to use techniques of this kind, you must also make it clear to the reader that you know your facts.

- Summarise the essential points at the outset so the reader knows where you are heading.
- Recapitulate essential facts where necessary to keep the threads untangled.

Summarise clearly all the main points you have made and the conclusions reached.

The language must serve the task

If you are writing on a science topic you will need to use the correct scientific terms – without being pedantic or showing off. Where you are dealing with any technical subject the proper terminology will demonstrate you basic grasp of the subject. But it is no good using technical terms unless you really know what they mean.

Any subject with its own 'jargon' has many traps for young players. If your subjects include such jargon, build up your own glossary of terms (either in note form or on a computer) and use this to refresh your memory constantly. By the time you get to examinations you must have a broad grasp of the terminology – and this is sometimes a language in itself.

Not only must you know this 'language' and the broader meanings and usage of the words, but you have to be able to spell them, too.

Use words as tools

Words are tools which should be used to cultivate meaning in a much broader sense than just stringing together a line of sausages.

The use of metaphor and simile, for example, are two devices that add colour and deepen meaning. In metaphor one uses words as pictures without likening them to the subject: 'The fat man floated exuberantly into the buzzing throng.' He didn't float, he only gave that impression. The throng wasn't buzzing, the mingled voices sounded like bees around a nest.

In simile, the subject is likened to something else to add to the meaning portrayed. 'She ran like the wind into a dark tunnel that glowed at one end like a lighted candle.' The difference from metaphor is that the two objects are linked by 'like' or 'as if' to act as a hinge on which the subject is articulated.

Be creative

Words are, after all, symbols that stand for things we commonly understand, and many words had their distant origins in metaphor and simile. So you can take a mundane word like 'brush' and apply it in a whole host of descriptive ways to mean a fox's tail, a mop of unruly hair, a passing touch (she brushed lightly against him), a bush on a heath etc. Once you start to think about the connections that link one word to the world of experience and perception you will start to see the possibilities of metaphor and simile, as well as the multiple meanings of most words.

Try crossword puzzles

If you would like to have a better appreciation of words, try puzzling out some crosswords, of which there are two kinds. The first is based on synonyms, that is words with the same meaning, or almost the same, as the clue. A good dictionary or thesaurus will get you started on these. For those who really want to stretch their minds, the cryptic crossword is the serious crossword fanatic's fare. Here the clue is 'encoded' to conceal or confirm the answer. There may be a key word in the clue which is a synonym for the answer, but the correct answer may also be contained in an anagram (letters jumbled together or making another word), segments of the word broken down into other meanings, or revealed through other clever tricks and devices.

The best-known cryptic crosswords appear in British newspapers but are reprinted around the world. The most difficult appears in *The Times*. Others, of varying degrees of difficulty, appear in the *Guardian* and the *Daily Telegraph*. *The Times's* crossword is the basis of an international competition and experts can sometimes solve the puzzle in a few minutes when it would probably take you many hours.

Crosswords have two attributes for developing language use. They focus on the multiplicity of meanings, a whole constellation of possibilities, that adheres to most words. And they reinforce correct spelling and usage. They are definitely a fun way to refine your spelling and relax at the same time. But they have another value, too. Only people who persevere and master the encoding system will succeed in getting the more complicated cryptic crosswords out – and it can be very satisfying the first time you beat the crossword compiler.

With cryptic crosswords, incidentally, you have to discern the way the mind of the compiler works. Each compiler has a number of quirks and deceptive tricks. In the *Guardian* newspaper, for example, each compiler has an assumed name so you know who you are pitting your wits against. This means you can pass one compiler over because you know you can never get anywhere with his or her brand of trickery. Or you can take up the challenge and battle on till you unravel the code.

Paragraphs

In the days when formal grammar was taught in schools it was customary to teach the basis of paragraph structure. Today, most of that formative work has been abandoned to the cult of 'spontaneity' or freedom of expression. There was much that was good in the old teaching principle, even if it tended to reinforce class divisions and stilt expression at first. Ultimately it led to an ability to communicate more logically and to a full mastery of the language.

Put simply, a paragraph had an opening statement or sentence which stated what it was about. The material was then presented sequentially until the end where the closing sentence acted as a lead-in to the next paragraph – to avoid mental hiccups in the reader. In the finished result the whole essay flowed from an opening paragraph which stated the content of the whole, through a logical progression through fact and argument with each paragraph seducing you into the next one, and concluded with a summary that set out the conclusions reached, perhaps after restating the essential facts.

This is little different from what we are proposing here, but our approach is less rigid and structured and so better able to embrace the foibles and creativity of the writer. Journalists, for example, don't work like that because they are limited by space and most 'journalese' is kept 'tight', without embellishments and the indulgences of recapitulation. But they do have one skill which is useful – lead paragraphs.

Lead paragraphs

A lead paragraph is a 'come on'. The object is to keep the reader 'on the bus' until the end of the report. If, however, the reader gets bored and gets off, he or she should have embraced the essential facts right up at the top of the story. A good lead paragraph, beneath a seductive headline, should compel you to read at least some of the story. If the journalist is very good you will read right to the end.

The lower you go down the scale of editors' perceptions of their readers' intellectual ability, the greater the skill applied to headlining and lead paragraphs. Compulsive readers don't need to be led by the nose into a story, but people who seldom read much need to be beguiled with vigour. Get hold of some popular newspapers to see how they go about this task, or decide from magazine cover headlines whether the stories interest you. You may learn something of use for your own work.

Construct your answer first

You should construct an essay or exam answer before you start writing unless you are dealing with areas such as maths, science or languages. And even there you will sometimes have to resort to composed responses to questions which follow the principles we are outlining here.

You need a road map to write a clear piece that progresses logically and comprehensively through the topic. Jot down on pieces of paper all the key points you can think of. Often this emerges in a logical sequence from the start but, sometimes, you may have to juggle the pieces until they form a clear pattern. Then, when you start writing, follow the road map and simply develop your theme by reference to the original headings or points. You don't need to go mad here – just make a list of, say, seven or ten points that will form milestones to be passed on the way.

Once you have these headings to 'trigger' a flow of ideas, and if you don't let your conscious mind intrude too much on the process, you should be able to roll through the essay or exam question by filling out, elaborating on, each point. Say what needs to be said, using any device of colour or story-telling to sustain or reinforce interest, go to the end and for heaven's sake *stop*. Don't be tempted to add on a few random and unrelated afterthoughts.

If you do have second thoughts, or facts or ideas occur to you after you have covered that particular point, reconstruct the page or pages you wrote originally. This will be difficult because of time constraints in an exam but is essential in essay writing. If the piece is written on a word processor so much the better, because you can edit or change the text as much as you like without tedious retyping.

How to persuade

When an essay topic or question calls for you to express a viewpoint or run an argument, logic must prevail. You are now moving into the more complex area of persuasion, in which the reader has to be convinced both that you know what you're talking about and that your case is sound. The reader will only be persuaded to your viewpoint if you can discredit his or her present position (as any debater knows well). To persuade – the once respected art of rhetoric – you must present facts and so order these that they support your ideas or contentions.

Facts are the foundations of your position, your hypothesis, and it is this central thrust of your argument that is the object of the exercise. To be successful you not only have to present the facts as you state your case, but you have to consider and deal comprehensively with the opposing position. This is like a game of chess. Unless you can discredit the antithesis, the opposite position, you do not win the argument and the reader is not convinced, so continues to hold his or her original viewpoint.

The purpose of setting essay topics that require the student to run an argument for or against a particular proposition is not to open up the views (or even prejudices) of the setter for modification but to demonstrate the ability of the student to argue coherently, present a logical and strong case and above all think clearly and even forcefully about the subject.

The essence of logic

A logical progression starts from the general, moves to the specific and finally closes with a conclusion that reinforces, strengthens, the writer's position. The specific details are where the facts speak for themselves and where each component part of the topic can be examined from either viewpoint. The view you wish to sustain is supported by the facts and the view you wish to discredit is undermined. The problem here is that there is always a temptation to put only part of the case, to select the facts that support your position and ignore those that erode the strength of your argument. A well-constructed argument is fair, covers all the facts adequately, and concedes points that cannot be argued against. Often, by making concessions which dispose of difficulties, you can actually strengthen your position by winning the reader over.

Logic demands you develop your theme systematically, moving from the initial general statements that are essentially simple to the details that are needed to demonstrate that your position can be sustained. In some cases, a logical progression may be chronological – in date order. The logical development of a theme in an essay, for example, could replicate the way in which a scientific discovery was made or emerged into human consciousness. Or it could start from the present state of the art and look at each component part through a magnifying glass, so ordering the parts that they fit together again afterwards. In other words, you move from the whole to its parts and reassemble the whole again at the end for it to be perceived by the reader in a different light.

The use of rhetoric

In the process of doing all this, don't forget the art of rhetoric. Any form of words that compels, persuades and rouses the emotions involves the skilled use of rhetoric and rhetorical device. There are many tricks of the trade: from the relatively simple repetition of key words or phrases to the use of a string of words starting with the same letter or sound, words skilfully arranged have the capacity to move and motivate people.

Edit your work

Having constructed your essay or exam answer, the job is not finished. Where possible, you need to edit, clarify, cut and polish your words. This *doesn't* mean that you have to write, write again, rewrite and endlessly reconstruct an essay The chance of it getting much better during such an assault is unlikely. The best written compositions tend to be the originals, and once heavy editing starts the original flavour can soon be lost. But there is always room for judicious pruning and clarification, and this depends on a careful re-reading of your work. Or rather two or three re-readings.

1. Re-read for sense, logic and coherence. Check that the facts are in order, the argument flows progressively, the conclusion is supported by the material in the middle, the detailed content, the facts.

2. Re-read and chop out all the unnecessary words, phrases or sentences that clutter up your meaning and intrude on clear thought. You will be amazed at how much superfluous verbiage you can edit out.

3. Check spelling, punctuation and presentation – the agreement of tense etc.

Check that your summary really does list all the key points dealt with in the detail. Ask yourself honestly at the close whether you believe you have made out a strong enough case to persuade your reader either that you know your stuff or that your proposition, your argument, has been sustained.

Writing that is enjoyable to read was, for the writer, a joy not a chore. A tedious and mundane piece of writing invariably comes from a student who was bored and uninterested in the topic. If the writer is fascinated by the facts and intrigued by the subject, his or her enthusiasm and 'fire' will illuminate the reader.

5. Developing an Exam Mentality

The purpose of exams

Exams are just the start of a long road to achievement. As you progress along your career path – or more likely paths – you will face many tests, some practical and others written. Developing the capability when young to handle exams competently will give you a head start.

Examiners set the question or exam topics to elicit specific areas of information from you. They want to know what you know and to assess the standard you have reached in a particular level of the subject. They work on the assumption that it is impossible to examine you in every aspect of the subject but that, if you don't know the questions in advance, you will have to cover the whole subject in revision and exam preparation. Clearly for some people this becomes a bit of a gamble.

If the exam paper contains those questions which the student can answer comprehensively rather than others where the student's knowledge is only marginal, the good marks obtained may give the erroneous impression that the student knew it all. Conversely, if the candidate is unlucky and the exam paper asks all the 'wrong' questions, a whole year's work can be 'wasted', in the sense that the required certificate, diploma or pass is not forthcoming.

The first point, then, about developing an exam mentality is to tackle your subject as a whole and not to select only those areas you feel convinced will be the focus of any exam.

What you need to show

The exam may be the ticket to future progress but, in the longer run, what you know may prove to be much more important. To master any area of knowledge, as we saw earlier, you need to be motivated by something more sustaining than just passing a few exams. You have to be interested in the subject to the point where learning occurs as a consequence of a need to know more. This places the emphasis on your selecting subjects, wherever, based on your personal interests and objectives and not according to some pattern determined by someone else – a parent, perhaps, or a university entrance prospectus.

While the examiner wants from you a demonstration of your competence in the subject, and an ability to handle the technicalities involved in exposing that knowledge, you want to learn, to attain a level of education that has the potential to fulfil your personal ambitions. Those two, possibly conflicting, positions have to be reconciled before you can be sure of performing according to the examiner's expectations. You want the examiner, or more broadly the examining institution, to ratify or certify your skills. Examiners want to maintain the standard, to certify only those people who, in their judgement, have attained a level of proficiency that justifies recognition.

Add to this another problem: few people really know what they know. It is only in the formal process of dragging their knowledge out into the light of day, as in a written or oral exam, that the knower discovers what he or she really knows, what has been absorbed in the back lanes and byways of the subject along the way. If you have no real means of knowing the level of your proficiency in this way, how can you prepare adequately for the exam?

The problem of nerves

Many students may not be able to perform well in exams. Their free flow of knowledge and the ability to express clearly what they know may be seriously inhibited by exam conditions and so they may give the impression that they are not competent when they really are. So factors of temperament and 'nerves' come into the equation, too. An essential part of developing an exam mentality is to be able to use the stimulus of the situation to key yourself up to maximise performance without allowing that tension to breed a level of anxiety or stress which becomes counter-productive. Or worse, metaphorically speaking, ties your hands behind your back.

A teacher I was talking to once about exam problems told me how she had dosed herself heavily with stimulants the night before an exam, sat up all night in a state of alarm swotting frantically and, without any structured plan, had appeared wide eyed and exhausted at the exam the next morning with her head in a total fug. That does not sound to me like a situation in which one is going to perform at all adequately.

Keep calm

The first quality one must develop is the ability to keep calm. The panic-stricken attitude may be as much a cultural expectation as an anxiety response. This culture of personal 'panic', which is evident in many important life situations from the job interview to appearing in court or making a public speech, is simply overcome by some clear thinking and self-training. The panic response has no value whatsoever. Being keyed up or nervous before a big event is fine, that ensures you function physically and intellectually at the peak of your capacity. It is this peak performance that we need to work on, like tuning a well-engineered motor engine.

Eliminate uncertainty

Uncertainty may take the form of not knowing the venue, what questions will be asked, whether your paper will be marked fairly, what people will say if you fail and so on. To overcome uncertainty and unfamiliarity you need to fill in as many of the gaps as possible. Ask questions, go and look at the exam venue, find out where the toilets are – or how your paper will be marked. The causes of much unjustified anxiety can be laid to rest quickly and permanently by a little exploration. Too many young people are frightened to take that step so they quiver with nerves instead.

We look at familiarising yourself with exam papers in detail in a separate section (p.48).

Know your physical cycles

Another part of exam trauma concerns your confidence in yourself and your fears that for some reason you may be under par physically and unable to perform to your best standard.

We are all subject to daily, monthly and seasonal cycles, and profoundly influenced by these unseen checkpoints. *Diurnal rhythms* determine that we reach a peak of activity and intellectual capacity usually around mid-morning. Our lowest ebb occurs around 3 am with another trough 12 hours later in the mid-afternoon. We peak again, depending on fatigue from the day's activities, in the evening before relaxing into a night's sleep.

These daily cycles may be affected by many outside factors: broken sleep, too much or too little sleep, sleep at the wrong part of the cycle, coffee or other stimulants, alcohol or other recreational drugs. Others include passing illness caused by bacterial or viral infections, travel (especially air travel through different time zones and the response to a seasonal change this can bring about), even sporting interests or commitments.

Yet, despite all these potential upheavals and the direct physical effects, top sports people manage to perform with almost surprising consistency in different time and seasonal zones after exhausting air travel. So can you when it comes to exam times. Knowing that diurnal rhythms have a powerful effect on your performance means you can maximise the beneficial effects by using a little common sense. But there's more.

Alongside the short-term, daily rhythms of life come the *monthly cycles* which, particularly for young women, may have a profound effect on their stamina and capabilities. An exam that coincides with the onset of menstruation for some girls can be a devastating event. Boys, too, perform better at some times of the month than at others, though the physical consequences are less evident.

Physical fitness

Add to these monthly cycles of peak and trough the day-to-day ups and downs of physical well-being and you will see that training for an exam is akin to training for the big race. In just the same way you need stamina, physical fitness, the ability to relax and sleep soundly, even a healthy diet and no debilitating abuses, dietary or otherwise. If you go into the exam tired or out of condition you cannot expect to do as well as you would otherwise have done.

That may sound like a statement of the obvious, but the teacher referred to above is stating the case for many students who seem to take satisfaction from displaying a panic response to what they may see as a ritual of admission to the adult world which *has to be* traumatic. Primitive peoples invented many bizarre forms of initiation into the adult community. From their perspective exams would be peculiar and impractical.

Here we have dozens, even hundreds, of initiates locked together in a room and watched over by a hawk-eyed elder while they wrestle with a sheaf of papers and torment their young minds into conformity. They are not permitted to speak or move around, and only under exceptional circumstances can they leave the room. Unless they subject themselves to this humiliation they cannot be admitted to the elect. If they succeed, the world is – in principle – at their feet and they are feted and rewarded with the symbols of attainment. But if they fail they face further humiliation and loss of social status.

The object of exam training for the candidate is to be able to perform to a good standard regardless of time of day, time of month or any other of the constant variables that afflict us all. Regardless of your state of mind, or body, you must be able to perform to order like a test cricketer or a top-seed tennis player. That requires training and the development of a strong mental attitude.

Rest and relaxation

All work and no play, they say, makes Jack, or Jill for that matter, dull.

Get away from books and word based knowledge and counter-act the mental demands with healthy, not overdemanding, physical activities. Don't go too far, though. Intense physical training can undermine the body's immune system, predispose you to illness and drain away energy from brain to feet, so to speak. The secret lies in balance. An excess of mental demand not counter-balanced by physical activity can be as destructive as the opposite state of affairs.

Students who pursue a sport or recreation that they enjoy and which provides a complete break from study will find themselves refreshed to the point that their minds are much sharper and their capacity for study greatly enhanced. It's not the long hours you put into study that yield results, it's the *quality* of the work that you do for certain periods. Twenty minutes of clear-headed discussion about a topic with an informed teacher could be worth three days of tedious and probably half-conscious reading. A 30-minute TV documentary may drive home the essential and most interesting points far more effectively than reading and re-reading 30 pages or partly illegible notes.

So the most vital part of training for exams is to invest your time wisely and constructively. And part of that investment must be made in physical well-being as a basis for mental function.

Mental fitness

We have already said that an essential part of the exam training schedule is to familiarise yourself with anything and everything about which you are uncertain or anxious, and this is especially true of the exam paper.

Practice papers

Most teachers in the run-up to exams provide students with earlier exam papers to use for practice. This is a good idea, especially where these papers have been selected for specific reasons. For example, the teacher may know that certain questions are likely to be repeated, or that some exam papers are more representative than others or that some students have a poor understanding of a particular topic. Teachers, too, have a vested interest in the good performance of students under exam conditions.

But the teacher proffering past exam papers, who was probably not involved in setting the exam, may be wrong. To overcome further uncertainty you should track down earlier exam papers in your subject in the library or wherever they are retained on file. By becoming conversant with the form of the exam, the way in which questions are framed and the answers required to gain full marks, much anxiety about the exam will be relieved.

You can practise answers, have them marked where possible or check the results against model answers. All this 'familiarity' will give you a strong sense of relief when you pick up the real exam paper and it is simply a repeat of what you already know and have practised repeatedly. Instead of approaching the examination like the Lottery and just praying that your numbers will come up, you will know exactly what answer is required and – provided you are not too apprehensive or lacking in personal confidence – you can rattle off the right reply.

How an exam is marked

When the *rite de passage* of the exam is over, examiners are confronted with a pile of handwritten papers which have to be marked, and as assessors, themselves helped by notes from the exam setters and model answers, perhaps where there is no fixed answer (as in a language or maths/science topic), they will try to allocate marks for clearly discernible facts, things you can confidently put a tick against. When you get into the more subjective areas of ideas or argument, the marking process becomes more difficult and the papers may be check-marked by a second person to attempt to achieve consistency of marking. Because of this, the student who is able to discern the examiner's purpose in asking a question, and pinpoint exactly what the question is seeking to elicit in response, has a better chance of collecting more of those ticks. A bit like a cryptic crossword, really.

Set or fixed answer exams are easy to mark. The answer is either right or wrong and there are no hard decisions to make. They are easier for the candidate, too, because you usually have a fair idea of how well you are doing during the exam.

The more complex 'open-book' or calculator- or computer-based exams may raise different issues which we will not explore here because we are dealing with the science of performance rather than specific examination styles and techniques.

There are also, of course, assessment techniques which seek to correct any obvious imbalance in performance between essay marks, teacher assessments of classroom activity and exams. These are designed to give a fair appraisal of the student's grasp of the subject by removing many of the distorting, or potentially disrupting, aspects discussed earlier.

What we propose to do in the next chapter is to develop a system to maximise your ability to recall and present what you *really* know.

6. The Science of Swotting

Draw up a timetable

In Chapter 1 we looked at different ways of notetaking. Whichever way you chose, start your *exam* preparation by making out a timetable. This gives you a countdown to the big day. On the timetable record your exam dates and times and the intervening time available. Block out at least *two days* before the exams start as a rest break. One student I remember decided to go off on holiday for two weeks before exams and he took no books or work with him. On his return he read through all his notes and pointers just once and went cheerfully like a sheep to the slaughter. He passed handsomely – but some of his frantically swotting peers were not so fortunate.

One young woman student fell madly in love just before the end of term and lost all interest in everything except the object of her affections. The couple spent the entire two weeks gazing soulfully into each other's eyes and mooning around the university grounds or along the river. Nothing could have been further from their minds than swotting – and they probably burned some midnight oil along the way. But they, too, both passed their exams with good results.

Clearly you have to allow for your temperament and inclinations, but the important point is that you should turn up for the exams fresh and fit, not in the last stages of a swot hangover.

Organise your notes

We established in the previous chapter that the thrust of examination strategy is to elicit from the student sufficient hard facts to demonstrate that he or she knows and understands the essential elements of the subject at the level required. How you organise your notes and 'recoverable information' is the key to preparing for exams. And the key to organising your notes into a mental pattern that you can draw on in the exam is to identify the information that is essential.

Without being too rigid about this (because subjects vary in scope and structure), take, say, four A4 lined pages and work through all the relevant notes you have (however detailed or contracted), noting everything you think is important *in outline*. When this is done – during which time you will have read right through the notes looking for specific facts rather than trying to retain a mountain of pointless data – use a marker pen to highlight a few key words of all the most valuable points you need to remember. Don't go mad. Stick strictly to the essentials.

Do this for each subject – very carefully laying out the material with plenty of white space. You will then have compiled a digest of the vital information represented by a few words for each topic or main point. Go through the sheets again and edit out all the dross – everything that you finally judge *doesn't really matter.*

You finish up, for argument's sake, with 16 pages of information and a lot of words picked out with the highlighter.

Now comes the hard bit.

How do you memorise?

First decide whether you are a parrot or picture person. Some people recall facts as a consequence of repetition and they remember the strings of words that make up the data, rather like a computer. Others have a photographic memory and recall patterns, shapes and pictures in a whole frame, so to speak. For our purposes it doesn't matter how you remember, just as long as you recognise how best your memory functions, because in the exam you will have to recall those key points to regurgitate the information that answers the questions.

The basis of the system proposed is that, having re-read your notes, you have to some degree refreshed your memory about the original input of information, whether lesson or lecture. Somewhere in the darker recesses of your mind it is all there. The problem is getting at it, like using a file name to locate material stored on a hard or floppy disk. Well, that's roughly what we are going to do: set up 'file names' for everything you may need to recall.

Many students, faced with a sea of information when revising, fly into a panic when they can't recall all the information at the drop of a hat or when asked a question. The mind computer whirrs and grinds but nothing comes out, because they are looking for a mishmash of facts rather than one word, the file name. Had they had such a handle to get hold of, the information would flow out unchecked, provided they were prepared to respect and use the computing power of the mind.

When the file is opened or 'triggered', whether the data flow spontaneously in strings of words or via a visual image, doesn't matter, as long as the system works.

Let us go back to that sheaf of abridged notes or key points.

However good your memory, there's no way you'll remember that lot in its entirety and be able to parrot it off or picture it under exam conditions. So it has to go through another refining process first. This time we're going to reduce it even more ruthlessly, onto one well-spaced page.

A way of remembering that works for you

If you have a picture memory, that is you recall by forming a mental picture of an arrangement of words or symbols, this final contraction needs to be set out in a particular way. If, however, you only need to trigger strings of words, you can adopt whatever arrangement makes it possible for you to memorise accurately all the file names, the triggers.

One pattern I found effective was to draw a neat circle in the centre of the page and write in capitals the subject title. From this hub radiated a series of spokes ending in more slightly smaller circles. Other longer lines led from the hub to an outer ring of circles and for each of these circles there were another two or three smaller subordinate circles.

In the inner ring of circles, write just one word – one word only – that becomes the trigger, the file name. These are, say, the seven or eight most vital keys. Into the circles of the outer ring, perhaps another seven or eight, write one word to represent the main but subsidiary pointers. And in the subordinate rings that connect to the outer circles, add one-word pointers that represent key elements of that subsidiary topic.

What you now have is a visual representation, a pattern, that fully summarises your subject area and gives you a way of accessing your mind to dredge up the information you need under exam conditions. The hard part is that you have to be able to recall exactly the single sheet 'pattern'.

Regardless of how you recall information, this is not as difficult as it appears at first sight, though it may require some tedious repetition until you can reproduce it exactly on paper and 'fix' it totally in your mind. Then you go into the exams with, say, four of these 'patterns' ready for instant recall and you make absolutely no effort to recall anything else until the big day. As long as you can retrieve the single sheet of headings, the rest (trust me) will inevitably follow, provided, of course, you are not physically or emotionally exhausted by swotting excessively, hung over, sick or in a blind panic.

The secret of using such a system is to get it down to the absolute minimum. The points sparkle out of your mind like the flashing of a diamond.

There is one last step which is completed when you are actually in the exam. Having read the exam paper carefully, draw on a sheet of paper your *aide mémoire*, the code sheet that is going to give you access to all those files stacked away in the hard (or floppy) disk of your mind. Once this is down on paper the effort of recall is over. All you have to do now is fit this pattern to the fabric of the exam paper and allocate the right triggers to the right question.

Of course this does not work for maths, languages or some science subjects which are technically complex. (We'll deal with the 'pure memory' subjects shortly.) But it will work for English, history, geography etc. Trust me! On second thoughts, rather than trust me, trust your own mind.

If you have any doubts about this approach, test it for yourself in end of topic test or mock exam. It works best if you are 'stressed out' by the exam situation and your performance is enhanced by the competitive and chemical responses of your body which act on mental function. And it should teach you the vital lesson that

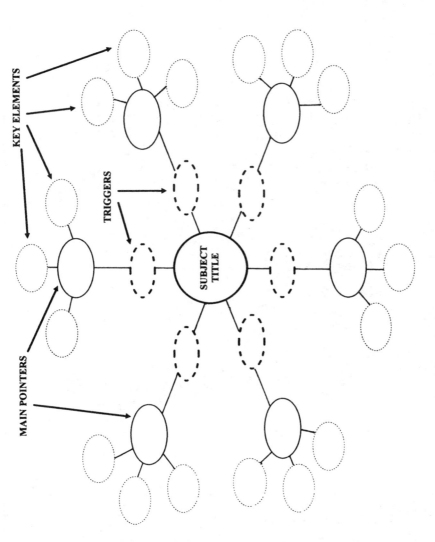

KEY ELEMENTS

TRIGGERS

MAIN POINTERS

SUBJECT TITLE

How to create your own memory aid

An example of a history memory aid

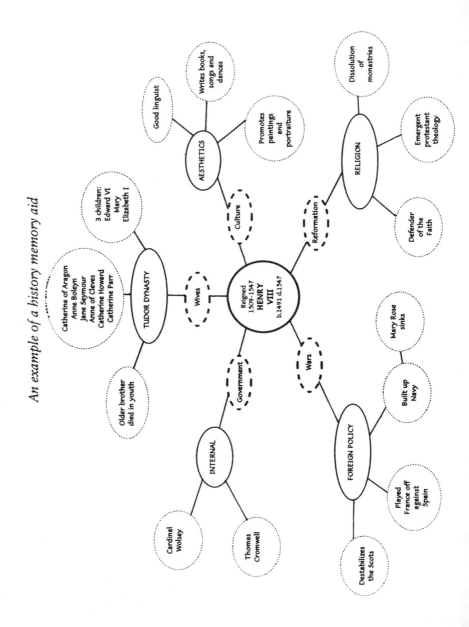

you don't know what you know until you put pen to paper.

The other element you may have to practise is compressing this information into just a few key words. It sounds easier than it is and there are a few tricks that can help here.

First, choose words to which you respond *emotionally*. If an emotive word is used it calls up a feeling, something that reaches beyond a cold intellectual response and involves your emotions in a certain (but probably indefinable) way. Second, the word must represent the topic area that it is to trigger in your mind. Wholly unrelated words will not have the same effect.

For example, you are taking a modern history exam and you wish to recall a 'file' about the Vietnam War. Where relevant you could use key words like bloodshed, defoliant, mines, choppers. All these words conjure up pictures related to a range of inputs from newspapers, TV or reading, and they trigger at once a whole constellation of ideas and facts. They have the effect of making the mind 'race' into the topic with spontaneous force, mainly because you have feelings, emotions, about many of these things.

The tough part of your task, however, is to represent a wide body of information with very few words. So the choice of those key words is critical in creating the flow of data on to the screen of your conscious mind.

As a second example let us use a classical topic like Shakespeare. You are going to be examined on the play *Twelfth Night*, which you studied for one term in great detail. The examiner wants to ascertain, first, whether you are familiar with the storyline and the characters in all their complexity. But he will also slip in a question that tests your understanding of Shakespeare's view of his world and his morality. How do you tackle a subject like that?

The central characters will lead to the 'also-rans', so focus on the 'big time'. These could be named in the outer ring of the diagram, with subordinate points about their roles flowing out further as before. In the inner rings, you will want to place triggers to recall the central and developing themes of the play – morality, conformity, justice, humour, trust, love, jesting, pride (or what you will). These abstract 'ideas', when linked with the play, will trigger thoughts of how the author and the main characters 'saw' these elements, and how you yourself interpreted the play and its relevance for your perceptions of the modern world.

The moment you focus on the word pride, for example, you will recall the fall of the tragic Malvolio at the hands of mischievous Maria. Your mind will (should?) race into a whole set of related ideas about the ruthless baiting of the old fellow and his inevitable downfall. Did he bring it on himself? Or was he the victim of cruel humour? What is the function and value of humour in human relationships? Was Sir Toby Belch, saint, villain or just a shallow layabout? Did the timid ranting of Sir Andrew Aguecheek, and his gullibility, say anything useful about the human condition? And how did all this fit with the political and romantic central theme?

You can get as abstruse as you like once these memories start to shower like mental confetti over your exam desk. As you start to force these ideas into some sort of order, you will along the way no doubt remember some of the brilliant language used to engineer or describe the wayward encounters of the play.

If you were fortunate enough to have a teacher who was able to pass on a love for the genius of Shakespeare you will relive and even savour the linguistic delights to a point where you may have to pinch yourself and get back down to earth in the exam room. It is that kind of involvement and enthusiasm which generates the best work, which is precisely why a subject that bores you stiff should be abandoned at the earliest possible moment in favour of something that fires your imagination.

Maths and the sciences

If you are taking exams in technical subjects, like maths and sciences, you may be able to use this system up to a point. It will be helpful both for remembering the fact-based material and for recalling key formulas or mathematical techniques. Otherwise, you will just have to practise each process and formula until it is firmly fixed in your mind through repeated use. Even then you can use 'triggers' to help in the fixing process.

Languages

In the case of a language, the best way to remember is to *use*. Time spent in a language lab is worth any amount of formal teaching. And a focus on colloquial communication is invaluable in giving purpose to the more formal grammar and vocabulary building process. Better still, a visit to the subject country is the best of all ways of learning a language because you are then setting your understanding of the language against the culture and environment of the people who use it.

A language (with the exception of Latin) is a living, evolving means of communication, and the more you can breathe life into learning it, the better. Today there are many opportunities to move beyond the language lab to reality – exchange visits and holidays, to name just two. If you grab hold of them you learn fast. Nothing reinforces vocabulary like making mistakes, and if you give native speakers (at home or in the country of the language) licence to correct you as you go, you will remember best those lessons where you were embarrassed by a stupid error. So, instead of poring over text books and learning lists of words, get out and *talk*.

Exams, too, may have an oral element and be designed to test both word discrimination and your ability to go beyond mere comprehension to communication. Whatever way you finally digest your material, you have to devise a formula *that works for you*. That means you may have to experiment until you find the right pattern. But remember that the process may be enhanced and more effective under real exam conditions than otherwise.

Back to recall

Part of all the compressing of information can be done as you work through the subject during the school or academic year. The object is to reinforce the key elements progressively, discard the unnecessary and generate a growing involvement in the subject that carries you along and energises your work. Ideally, you should reach the point where you live and breathe your subjects and are driven by fascination, not examination.

This compelling or even consuming interest spurs retention of information to the point where, if you could somehow retrieve everything you have learned, you would be amazed at the sheer volume of files tucked away in memory, in this case random access memory.

Facing the test

Your swotting is finished, the memory sheets are by now firmly implanted in your mind and you can recall them *completely* at will. The urge to read over your notes is nagging away when you see peers strung up in intellectual knots trying desperately to remember detail. For one horrible moment you wonder whether this is not all an illusion and whether, when the chips are down, the command processor (to maintain our metaphor) will fail.

That is the final key – self-confidence. You have to believe in yourself, in the capacity of your mind to proffer the information at will and in your own ability to translate that into legible words, well spelled and punctuated.

Stick to the golden rules.

1. Never, never swot the night before. If possible, take a total break two or three days before the exams start and forget everything, everything.

2. Trust yourself.

3. Don't fret if you can't sleep before a big exam – but don't lie in bed trying to recall everything you know. You may crash the computer with overload.

4. Keep fit and get adequate exercise in the run up to the exams. But don't overdo it. And if you begin to feel 'stressed out' you're allowing emotion to drown out reason. If you have followed the plan properly there's nothing to worry about, so go for a long walk in peaceful surroundings and empty your mind.

5. Last of all, don't ever open a book, let alone your notes, on the

day of the exam. If you don't know it now, you never will. (But, of course, you really do.) We will allow you one small concession, however. You can take a quick refreshing peep at your 'trigger' sheets, just to reinforce the patterns in your mind.

A final word of warning. On the day of the exam, and preferably not in the days before, don't attempt to reproduce facts flowing from the *aide mémoire* on paper. This is because the mind, or some people's minds, seem to have an erase function. Once the material in your mind has been triggered to flow into consciousness it seems to be purged because it is now offloaded on to the paper. Focus on the triggers by all means, but leave them to do the work when the time really comes.

7. The Big Day

Keeping calm

After enough recreation, rest and sleep you are ready for the start of your exams. Maybe you didn't sleep as well as you would have liked because you were a bit apprehensive, to say the least. So let's go back over two key points. If you're tense before the first exam, that's only natural. The effect of exam nerves, or any form of anxiety about performing in public or competitively, as we saw earlier, is necessary. It is only natural to be tense before the first exam. Exam nerves, or any form of anxiety about performing in public or competitively, as we saw earlier, are necessary to key you up and maximise your performance. Look on these feelings as beneficial, an advantage, not a problem.

Second, don't stand around outside the examination venue struggling to remember information or, for that matter, your single page 'triggers'. Trust your mind to deliver when the time comes and don't worry.

Certainly, a lot hangs on your performance over the next few days, but worrying is not going to add anything to the task of displaying what you know. Now you must put theory into practice and show your confidence in your ability to handle exams calmly and carefully.

What sort of candidate are you?

Some students, faced at last by that dreaded exam paper, behave like a starving person eating their first meal for a week – they turn over the question papers, try to read them through thoughtfully, but then throw caution to the winds as they start writing frantically. They may still be writing at an ever-increasing pace when the exam is over. Others 'freeze' and turn pale as their minds go blank. They drop their pens, shuffle their papers, sigh, and cast desperate, sidelong glances at their more fluent peers. Having spent too much time wasting time they finally, nervously start to write. They, too, are still writing at the end. Then there are the students who bemoan their bad luck that the questions they *could* have answered were not asked.

If you recognise yourself (or, indeed, your friends) in any of these categories you need to know that these are all failures of self-confidence – not of knowledge. If you have followed the plan outlined in Chapter 6 these forms of panic need not plague you for a moment. You know what you have to do – stay in control. You need to read the entire exam paper (or at least those sections which apply to your topics) slowly and carefully. Decide which questions you are going to answer, recover the file manager and get it down on paper so that you are armed with all the triggers necessary to tackle the questions. Sort out which material you need for each of the questions you have selected, allocate the time available intelligently, and start writing without further delay.

Selecting and answering questions

Selecting the questions needs care, too.

Obviously you are going to choose those topics where you feel most comfortable. If you have done your revision efficiently, however, you should be able to handle almost any question. Some questions, perhaps because they touch on your interests, will obviously appear more promising. *Do these first.* There is no rule which says you have to answer the questions in any particular order. Your task is to persuade the examiner that you know your stuff and feel confident about your knowledge and ability.

Having selected the questions you prefer to answer, read the question carefully, *then read it again* until you are certain what the examiner wants to elicit from the answer. *Answer only the question* and don't get drawn into blind alleys and side issues. When you re-read your answer later before handing in the paper, you should be able to put ticks against each of the points that will earn marks. (More of this later.) Keep responses as brief as possible and to the point. There are no marks for quantity, only quality. Completed exam papers are not weighed by the kilo, they are *weighed up*.

Lay out each answer clearly, with plenty of white space, to make it easy to edit and add to where necessary. Make it as easy as possible for the exam markers to do their work – generous margins, legible handwriting, an opening paragraph that summarises or states the case, key points briefly listed or stressed. For emphasis you can use capital letters or underlining.

Pacing yourself

If you are wearing a wrist watch, take it off and place it on the desk where you can see it. This way, you won't get so absorbed in what you are doing – and that happens often – that you forget the time and finish too late to read over your paper, edit and correct spelling and punctuation. In the re-reading at the close of the exam you may need or want to add a few points that you missed. While these may be out of sequence in the answer they can still earn you marks. So leave space after each question, say half a page, just in case.

Keep a wary eye on the time because you may be surprised at how quickly it passes. If you find the first question out of four has used up a third of your time, calculate the time remaining for each of the other three answers.

Better still, don't allow that to happen in the first place unless you see some advantage in such a strategy. Some questions may carry more marks than others (this is indicated on the exam paper) so you may prefer to go for the big time first!

People work at different rates. If you are a fast worker you may also be a careless writer, so be aware of this and allow more time for checking and correction at the end. If you are a slow worker don't waste time on roughing out notes for an answer or dithering about which questions to answer. Self-discipline now is vital if you are to keep up with the quick workers. Slow and steady may win the race, but an exam is invariably a race against time for anyone who knows their subject well.

Having placed your watch on the desk, get in the habit of glancing at it frequently to see if you are on schedule. If you are not, take corrective action to ensure that you don't run short of time to answer *every* compulsory question as comprehensively as possible.

These may seem like statements of the obvious, but it's amazing how many students don't think about the *technique* of writing an examination paper. They focus only on the knowledge they must regurgitate, not how they are going to do this to the best of their ability.

Writing the answers

Use your memory sheet (*aide mémoire*, trigger pattern, whatever you choose to call it) to structure the answers. Having decided which key words embrace the material for the question you are going to answer, allow the points to trigger the flow of ideas into your mind. If you have followed the system correctly, and mastered the technique by practice, the answer should simply issue from your pen without too much conscious interference on your part. After all, you know the information, your time has been sensibly allocated, the sequence and structure of the answer is already on paper in front of you, so you can't lose your way. It is now simply a matter of getting on with the job.

When you believe you have answered the question, check back briefly to see whether you have included all the key points from your memory sheet. If you have to add another point out of sequence at the end of the question, you can always label it (for argument's sake) 'A' and indicate where it belongs in the full answer.

Trust your mind

At this point you're going to ask: What if I can't remember? What if all this stuff *doesn't* flow from my pen and I'm sitting there like a stuffed owl staring into space?

How do I know this system really works in an exam?

That, of course, is where self-confidence comes in. By the time you reach the examination room you should be convinced that this plan is going to work for you – because you have completed enough dummy runs to know that your mind can work like a computer if you just let it. And because it has worked well for other people in the past.

(Using this system, I obtained four distinctions in my first-year exams at university, racing through the questions without any hesitation. I had no means of knowing whether it would work in practice because I had never used it before, either, but I felt comfortable with the theory.) Trust yourself, *trust your mind*.

Once you have demonstrated the effectiveness of working in this way, exam technique will be at your fingertips, so to speak. That will remove a huge hurdle in the study process in succeeding years – and for any other time later in life when you are to be examined formally, perhaps in the armed forces or public service – because you will know exactly how to get good results.

'Fair enough, but what do I do if I really can't remember?' you may insist.

Beating the block

If this happens, you are not letting your mind work for you. The short answer is to leave sufficient space and simply go on to the next question. Sometimes, for a variety of reasons, the mind 'blocks' and the flow of ideas or information checks temporarily. It's a condition well known to writers – writer's block. For them, the answer is to quit for a while, do something completely different, and just wait until the double-bind goes away.

In an exam you can't get up and walk around the block, so to speak, so you have to ignore the traffic jam and sidestep it by turning your mind to something completely different, another question. Once you relax again, you'll be able to go back – perhaps a bit apprehensively – to the original question, and you'll probably find the ideas flowing again.

Combating fatigue

One reason for writers' block may be fatigue.

A person's span of concentration varies. University lecturers often say that most students fade out after 45 minutes of lecturing, so two-hour lectures are counter-productive, even with a break in the middle. Depending on the level of interest and involvement, some people find their mind wandering after just 20 minutes. But some exams last for up to four hours. How can one sustain such intense concentration for that length of time? Because maintaining concentration is a critical element of passing exams and doing your best work.

First, there are the physiological factors. Did you have an adequate breakfast – enough to maintain an energy output for the period of the exam? If you're one of those people who starts the day with a cup of black coffee and a cigarette after a 'nightcap' when you went to bed, let's face it, you will flag after a couple of hours – however keyed up and anxious you are.

One answer is to use barley sugar, or anything sweet, to raise your blood sugar level when the first signs of fatigue or lack of concentration become evident. Another is to stop work and stretch, open up your shoulders and breathe deeply for a minute or two, long enough to break the physical tension of sitting huddled over a desk for a long time. Rotate your head and massage your neck and shoulders. Or lock your hands behind your head and press backwards several times. Stretch your legs out and rotate your feet. Do whatever works for you.

A better long-term strategy, however, is to eat breakfast so that you start out with the physical resources needed to sustain a long period of concentration.

If you are a coffee drinker, remember that the maximum effect of caffeine, the stimulatory effect, takes several hours to peak. There is no harm in using coffee as an aid provided you understand that, once the peak has been reached, there may be a trough later. If you use coffee late at night, you may not sleep well and could be tired for an exam in the morning. The day before the exam it may be sensible to avoid coffee after lunch. If you are against using stimulants of any kind you may ultimately perform better, but that depends on your individual physiology.

Another problem arises when you have two exams in one day. You may fly through the morning exam while you are at the peak of your daily cycle but, come the afternoon, you may be facing a marked downturn in energy and concentration. And this may be exaggerated by a good lunch which leaves you contented but brain dead.

Everyone has to discover what is best given their individual make-up, but one solution may be to have a light lunch followed by a quick nap somewhere peaceful. Half an hour is more than enough. You will most likely wake refreshed and a hot drink will probably get your mind up to speed again quickly.

Language exams

In language exams, you will probably have to face a conversation test. The examiners are well aware of how you feel and know how to make allowances for 'nerves' or the student's mind just 'going blank' at the wrong moment. The secret is to keep the conversation going – and you will be able to do that if you have practised and practised and practised so that some responses have become automatic.

If you are stumped by a statement from the examiner, ask him or her to repeat it to give you time to think. There is no time limit in most cases, so you can afford to take things step by step to show what you really know and the extent of your vocabulary and fluency.

You may also have to complete a listening or discrimination and comprehension paper. There is often a preliminary reading to allow you to familiarise yourself with the speaker's voice and intonation, and you only have to listen to this and relax. You will not be expected to understand every word, at least at school level, so concentrate on getting the subject matter and gist of the reading the first time round. You will then have a second chance to fill in some of the gaps.

If you are given any aids for the exam, use them intelligently rather than forgetting about them in the hassle of trying to listen to the spoken text. You may even be allowed to use a bilingual dictionary for some written papers, but don't waste too much time on this because, by the time of the exam, you should be familiar with most of the words used.

Maths and Science exams

In these subjects examiners often give credit for correct working, even though the answer may be wrong at the end, so all calculations and processes should be shown.

In maths, and in science for that matter, the clear logical presentation of your answer is vital, because you are convincing the examiner by mathematical argument and process, and your exposition should be just as clear as if you were answering in words. Explain what you are doing even if the process is not obvious. And wherever possible, show the examiner what you know, not what you can't remember.

In examinations on technical subjects always use the proper terminology. This shows you have immersed yourself in the subject and often acts as conceptual shorthand, saving a lot of time in unnecessary explanations. In these subjects there will be a heavy reliance on different forms of progressive assessment. There may be practical assignments, written tests, research papers done at home, even classroom discussions and the preparation of technical reports. The same basic rules of communication apply here but you will have to adapt and hone your skills to the needs of that particular subject.

In technical areas a simple clear diagram is worth a thousand words. Use illustration wherever possible to develop or reinforce what you are trying to convey in writing. Where you have access to specialised equipment and computer support, master the use of these aids early in the course and make the best possible use of their support potential.

With computers, for example, a great deal of software facility is often overlooked because a student doesn't take enough time to explore all the avenues. Much of the software in use now offers a range of graphs and charts as well as supporting analysis and ordering functions.

If you confront multiple choice exam questions, provided there is no penalty for a wrong answer, have a stab at every question, whether or not you are sure of the right answer. You could hit the jackpot with luck, or even judgement.

Assessing your performance

Let's assume you have finished the exam paper to your satisfaction, checked that all the key points have been included, corrected spelling and punctuation, and there are still a few minutes left. Don't rush to hand in your paper. Use *all* the available time productively. In this case, run through the paper from the start, mentally noting where you believe you have scored marks. This assessment, assuming it looks promising, will help build your confidence for other exams.

Check off against your memory sheet the points you included in the answers for later confirmation against your original sheet and your notes. Another benefit of doing this is to refine the memory jogging technique. You may find that certain key words worked better for you than others. Or that one particular arrangement or layout of the words worked better than another. You will have an opportunity to assess the system and develop it to meet your needs to best effect.

I well remember sweating over one key word I couldn't recall. Whichever way I looked at the memory sheet, it just wouldn't come back. When I checked against the original later, all the points were there just as they should have been. What I had forgotten was that three of my sheets had seven main points but one had eight. The answer was to fix on a standard number of points covering the likely exam topics and the main thrust of the course for each sheet – then I was certain.

Some examination rules

In most cases the exam hall is open about ten minutes before the scheduled time of the exam. Some examining authorities forbid a student to leave within, say, 30 minutes of the starting time; others will not allow candidates to leave until the scheduled end of the exam. If you have to leave permanently for any reason you must hand in all papers to the invigilator before you go. If you need to leave temporarily you will be escorted out of the exam room, and back.

If there is a separate book in which you are required to answer one or more questions, and you do not answer these questions, you should indicate on the cover that it has not been used but you must still hand it in with other completed work.

Most authorities forbid you to carry into the exam anything that may provide you with information to help in the exam. This includes books, notes, jottings or anything that could broadly come under the label of 'cheating'. There are exceptions, for example Theatre Studies notes on performances and set texts. You will probably have to hand these in with your answers.

You must not help another candidate, either directly or by allowing him or her to read what you have already written. And you must not accept such help from any other candidate. For the rest, you have to shut up, work fast and have a good-looking paper.

Most examining bodies allow the use of calculators, but you have to use your own. You will not, however, be permitted to take in a calculator with a cover that you can write on, or mark in any way.

Slide rules and compilations of tables are allowed if the syllabus says so. You may also use stencils with maths formulas provided they do not give you any advantage over other students. Specific products are usually approved by the examiners.

8. Getting Better at What You Do

Practice

Now that you have mastered the principles and technique of passing exams and writing top essays it is time to refine the process through practice and experience until you can always rely on performing to the very best of your ability. The basic principles of writing exams and essays will always be applicable to the more complex writing tasks that you will inevitably face in the world of work. Working life for most people involves some written material – reports, letters, presentations – and the better you are able to communicate in writing, the more competent you will be.

The basic principles set down in this book have armed you for these tasks, but practice makes perfect.

Read and listen

Along with practice, however, reading material produced by able communicators also helps to develop your appreciation of good writing technique and correct spelling and punctuation. What you learn from reading depends on your awareness and critical focus.

Most professional writers, be they TV or radio broadcasters or journalists, or authors of fact or fiction books, have mastered these principles so their work is on display for you as a model or standard of good communication. Regrettably, however, literary standards have slipped sharply in recent years in the press, though book publishers, particularly some British and American imprints, are still maintaining careful, and sometimes impeccable, standards. Though some journalists may survive in this language jungle despite their sins of ignorance, by and large communication skills – oral and written – will determine your career success.

In addition the tradesman, shop assistant or managing director all depend on their ability to get their point over to other people and reinforce that view by valid argument and imparting understanding. So the skills you develop now will underpin almost everything you do in the future, whatever your occupation.

Be self-critical

In reading and appreciating, even criticising, the work of others, you will discover that there are essentially two different types of people – *information takers* and *opinion makers*. The first group are the consumers of mass media products who mainly absorb but seldom give out in any public sense. The opinion makers guide and develop, or even confuse or regress, popular thought – sometimes to serve vested interests.

Good communicators, if they demonstrate an ability to persuade as they inform, will go far in their careers and prove to be those who change society for good or ill. Such is the potential of powerful communication. The pen is indeed mightier than the sword.

Lifting your own game relies, first, on becoming an ardent self-critic. That does not mean cultivating a negative perception of your own abilities as a basis for self-denigration and loss of confidence. Rather it means you have to recognise your strengths and weaknesses and work at improving those areas where you are not performing as well as you could.

Self-criticism is a problem in some ways. An assessment of your own work may not be made on the same basis as that of another reader. Your perceptions, and self-criticism, may be based on wholly different premises because you are the communicator and the reader is the recipient of what you have to say. *You* know what you mean, but you have to convey that meaning, clearly, to the other person. So being the communicator or the one to whom the communication is being directed bring quite different perceptions to the meeting of minds.

Learn to handle criticism from others

Self criticism therefore has an important part to play in refining your work – but the criticism of others is much more to the point. This, too, raises difficulties, because some people – particularly where it concerns a creative act like writing – cannot handle criticism. These people tend to react to even well-meaning criticism (and not all of it *is* well-meaning) in one of two ways. Either they react aggressively and conclude that the critic is talking through the back of his or her neck, or they retreat into their shell and conclude that they are no good at what they do. What they do not do is see what can be learnt from the exercise.

When my first book was published it was savaged in a big feature article in the *Daily Telegraph* – my first ever major review, and I was devastated. I read and re-read the pompous opinions of a bombastic stuffed shirt and concluded, as young people do, that he must know what he was talking about. When the good reviews started to appear I soon realised that this critic had used the central theme of the book to parade a set of ultra-conservative prejudices that had little appeal for most other readers. When, finally, the book received an accolade from the most respected and professional critic of all, I was not only immensely relieved but rehabilitated.

None of us *likes* criticism, particularly when it is unjust or unfair (as it often is), but we have to be able to maintain a belief in ourselves despite all. That comes with experience.

There are times when school students are savaged by a particular teacher with whom his or her face does not fit. At university level, especially in postgraduate work, some students run off at a tangent to the conventional wisdom of their teachers and get put down ruthlessly for their insolence.

I remember giving a copy of a draft thesis to a lecturer to read, hoping to elicit from her some constructive comment. A few days later she tossed the typescript back to me with her eyes blazing: "Fascist pig!' was all she could offer. This was not only appallingly rude and intolerant, it was totally untrue and unjustified in every sense. The book, far from being fascist in tone, was liberal and progressive in every sense.

What seems to have happened is that the lecturer had stumbled

74

across a paragraph early in the manuscript which she had read out of context. From this, and having read no more, she 'threw a wobbler' as they say and threw the draft back at me unread. The moral of this tale is to evaluate the criticism and react to what is constructive if you believe the point made is valid.

Otherwise, cast it off.

How you handle criticism from others will in many ways determine the way in which your self-confidence develops. Harsh criticism tends to play on the mind and can undermine the creative process involved in good communication, so you have to develop what could be termed mechanisms for coping with this when it happens. One way to do this is to seek another opinion.

When unsolicited criticism, or the negative perceptions of someone in a position senior to you, cause you to stop in your tracks and wonder, after all, whether they may not be right and you wrong, get someone you trust and respect – and who feels the same about you – to read the material and comment. They may be too kind because they don't want to hurt your feelings, and you will be aware of this, but it may do wonders for rekindling your creative flame.

If you doubt yourself, others will doubt you, too. Believe in yourself and your abilities, and – perhaps surprisingly – you'll carry others along on the crest of that wave with you.

Develop self-confidence

Psychologists used to say that a feeling of superiority concealed an inferiority complex. Fortunately, psychology seems to have moved on a bit from this banal view. Certainly, there are people who suffer from a high measure of self-doubt, who bluster to cover up what they fear are their shortcomings.

The best way to get a confidence kick is to seek informed and balanced assessment of your work from people who are in a position to be fair and who invariably display good judgement. The best confidence builder of all, of course, is success and esteem. If your peers or seniors say your work is good, then you won't want to dispute that. But there is a problem inherent in this, too. Until you reach the cosy point where you can bathe in the praise of others, you have to have enough confidence in what you are doing to persist to the point of success. Too often other people don't really know whether the material they are reading is good or not.

Take as an obvious example the many best-selling books that were rejected over and over again by eminent publishing houses. The publishers, or more particularly their manuscript readers who report on projects, simply failed to see the value of the material. They may even have failed to perceive the quality of the writing or they may have simply looked at the sales potential and concluded the market was too small for such a work.

There are many surprising examples of this – *Watership Down* by Richard Adams became a classic of its kind. Another often rejected title, *The Peter Principle*, became common parlance when the book was finally published, and we still talk about the concept to explain managerial incompetence.

So beware of trite critics spouting meaningless words.

It may even be that, in the final analysis, only you really understand the value and excellence of your work – and had you lost confidence in that, it might never have reached the audience it deserved or earned the concomitant respect. Believe, then, in yourself.

Gateways to your future

The foregoing has been an attempt to relate the mundane work of essays and exams to the wider world of achievement and modern society. As the information highway assumes an even greater role in our lives we will be turning back from the world of TV images to the communicative potential of the written word. Presumably, some kind of spoken and visual form of immediate communication will develop in the future to build on the global networks now being established through computers linked to a modem. In the interim, however, writing skills will continue to be vital.

The assessments and marks won from school and university work are the first outside and, hopefully, impartial views of your ability, your first real brush with critical acclaim or condemnation. They are also gateways through which you must pass to attain your future career options, so they are going to affect your life profoundly for good or ill.

Because of this, you must maximise your potential by learning the language of educational communication on which exam and essay success rests. In the concluding chapter we pull together all the essential points that have been made so far to provide a working framework for developing that potential fully.

Conclusion

The following is a letter written to the editior of a provincial Australian newspaper.

> Wouldn't it be nice if all exams became open-book exams? For many students, the reduced stress would mean a truer indication of their learning. Also examiners could no longer rely on those memory testing questions. Rather, their questions might check how well students can find relevant information and how well they understand it.
>
> Wouldn't it be nice if the magic of statistics was no longer used to select students for university courses? Each university department might have to state any compulsory subjects, as well as a pool of acceptable and equally weighted extra subjects, students need for entry into their courses.
>
> Wouldn't it be nice if exam questions were 'authentic' in that they related to the kinds of problems and tasks faced by workers in the real world?
>
> Wouldn't it be nice if exams revealed those students who are good at creative and critical thinking? Are exams producing students who can think in these ways, which are so vital in this rapidly changing and competitive world?

John Langrehr

Anyone reading this book will probably agree with Langrehr's view. For my part there was a compelling urge to change the word 'nice' to 'better' and move a couple of commas, but that is pedantic. He is right, of course, but we don't live in an ideal world and are unlikely ever to do so.

In the meantime, what can we do? Consider this extract from a newspaper exam guide, produced mainly by curriculum experts and educators, which offered some useful pointers. The examiners and moderators of one external assessment board are said to:

> work to make sure that assessments match subjects studied and that they are fair and reasonable. Trick questions and deliberate traps are not part of the processes used... It is a requirement... that assessments and examinations will be designed to give every student the best opportunity to show what they have learnt.

That, too, is the ideal but, sometimes, your performance or that of your assessors may not fully reflect the ideal. This is why *you* have to make sure that your performance realises the best effort of which you are capable.

One curriculum officer advises students facing assessment for practical subjects like health education or home economics to prepare material for final assessment with great care. Though requirements differ, final exams are seldom demanded. He says you should:

1. Finish uncompleted work thoroughly.

2. Prepare the folder containing completed assignments, tests, independent studies or negotiated contracts and any other relevant or required material with care.

3. Label all sections clearly so assessors can find specific material easily.

At this point let's list and summarise the key points of the secrets of exam success, foundations of a good essay and how to win marks the easy way.

Ten secrets of exam success

1. Develop skills in written and verbal communication.

Without the ability to communicate what you know clearly and competently you will be penalised from the start. But communication goes further. You have to be able to persuade, run a strong argument and deal with counter-arguments effectively. Without excellence in communication your career will be disadvantaged in a world that is becoming increasingly dependent on the use of language.

2. Motivation is the essence of learning.

And motivation flows from interest, a compelling interest, in what you study. Whatever the source of that drive which pushes you forward and gives you the energy and commitment to work well and competently, you will not perform well if the subject bores you mindless. To maximise the potential of study, select subjects that you are motivated to learn about through interest.

3. Plan the school or university year.

Do this in the light of other personal commitments, and don't bite off more than you can chew. There is much more to the intelligent process of study than bulldozing your way intellectually through mountains of work. We are talking about a developmental experience, on in which you are laying the foundations for your later interests, career and personal potential. Setting out at the beginning of the academic year to plan your workload, allocate available time to best effect and provide for physical fitness and adequate rest and recreation is a part of that experience.

4. Organise notes and learning materials.

You must be able to retrieve the information easily and quickly so that when the time comes, revision and the preparation of memory joggers is simplified. For the system recommended in this book you need to reduce the volume of notes and increase the time you spend listening and thinking about your subject. By working towards a one-page summary of everything you know about one subject, and memorising these trigger points before the exam, you have everything you need to retrieve the data you need from your own mind.

5. Discard the dross.

Concentrate on what is relevant in all your learning. You cannot hope to bring back to consciousness everything you know, or have assimilated, during the year. Don't even try to do that, but trust your mind to deliver the flow of associated ideas when needed. At the same time you can make the process simpler and more straightforward by not cluttering up your mind with piles of irrelevant information that will neither serve your interests nor add to your marks in an exam. How do you discriminate between the dross and the relevant? Be guided by compelling interest.

6. Take time to think, reason and apply your own judgement.

This applies as much to essay writing and exam technique as to the task of learning what you need and want to know and to 'real' life. A good teacher develops the student's own capacity for intelligent thought and reasoning and it this quality above all others that the educational experience seeks to emphasise. At the most extreme, if your teacher is a confirmed creationist and a member of some charismatic religious order who is misguided enough to attempt to misdirect his or her students, you have to be able to see beyond the propaganda to a rational and acceptable view of the world.

7. Teach yourself to manage exams.

Develop competence in the techniques of working within a fixed time-scale, presenting your answers in a visually attractive and clear manner and thus maximising your marks. As in most areas of life, there are tricks of the trade and simple practical techniques which, when applied to the examination room, can maximise your results.

8. Revision is affected considerably by the methods employed.

Refine your swotting technique until you revisit only those facts, ideas and processes you need to excel. Organising your mind is more important than organising your notes and files. Once your mind is in order, the rest of the retrieval process is a breeze. The critical point here is to create a system, a formula, a technique, *that works for you* and is easy to use.

9. A degree of exam tension keys you up.

Being nervous gets you to the point where your mind's alive and working well, so use this tension to good effect. Going beyond that stage to blind panic means that you are not confident in your own ability and have not trained yourself appropriately for the task before you. You are probably overtired and cannot perform well because your mind is not sufficiently clear to disgorge the facts you need.

10. Be realistic about your shortcomings and limitations.

Work during the year on removing all the handicaps to good performance. Teachers or tutors may highlight some of these problems but, in the end, only your self-analysis and self-criticism will refine your exam skills. This also means that you must not overreact to external criticism nor become self-critical to the point of destroying the basis of your self-confidence. While nothing succeeds like success, nothing is so galling as failure.

Three foundations of a good essay

Essays are quite different, being a reflective process in which you have the time and resources to reveal your skills in a medium wholly removed from the pressure and artificial environment of the examination room. Because of this, the standards required in an essay – of communication skill and knowledge – are much higher.

There are three foundations of a good essay.

1. Write clearly, as briefly as the subject dictates, and accurately – with good spelling, grammar and punctuation. The language of the essay should never get in the way of the information you wish to convey or the argument you are using to persuade your reader that one viewpoint is preferable.

2. State your subject matter, your case or the structured plan of the essay at the outset and then summarise and reinforce your key points at the end. Readers may have short memo-

ries, become distracted, read a part of your work then pick it up again later, or just let their attention wander. Help, guide and strengthen the reader's perceptions and responses.

3. Use facts, hard information, that are so interesting they are compelling. The essay that bores is the essay that fails to communicate effectively. Essay markers can be excused sometimes for letting their attention waver, so give them something to think about. No good teacher wants you simply to regurgitate the facts imposed on you during the coursework. Introduce your own research, a fresh view, or a challenging argument, and you can lead your reader by the nose.

Winning marks

To end with, some pointers to winning marks in an exam, and even an essay for that matter, the easy way.

Assessors look for specific points in an essay or exam paper which are milestones along the path to understanding. So identify those points as the course proceeds – if in doubt, ask the teacher or lecturer for an assessment of the points that matter – and make sure these are highlighted in your essay or exam answer. You can underline them, write them in capital letters or pick them out with a coloured pen.

A word of warning, however. Exam markers are as individual and as varied in their views as students, so do not insult their intelligence. Set your key points within the broader context or argument in which they have clear relevance and meaning, and try to soar like an eagle rather than gobble like a turkey.

Get your reader or exam marker excited by the material you offer, and his or her marking hand tends to become more flamboyant. You make an assessor angry or exasperated, or doubting the rewards of teaching as a career, at your peril. The best and simplest formula for success is competence – solid factual knowledge and clear exposition. If you get *that* right, the rest should follow, with exam success and essays that win top marks.

Index